The F

MW00916231

Bill Orr, III

* * * * *

Copyright 2012 by Bill Orr, III

1

The Preferred Way

Dedication

This book is dedicated to the people that believe in me. I have set lofty goals at different points in my life. My Mother always believed I could do anything, if I put my mind to it. Her assumption was finally proven correct after achieving the Dean's List along with several academic awards and earning a Bachelor of Science degree in three years. It was an outstanding experience for my mother and me, especially when you consider that worked full time to support myself and pay the costs of attending college.

I would also like to dedicate this book to my recently-departed friend and mentor, Louis. He always served as a good sounding board and his wise counsel will be sorely missed. Finally, but most importantly, this book is dedicated to my beautiful daughter, who has achieved what most people only dream about. I am very proud of her and love her dearly.

One of the most important lessons that I have learned is that if you believe in yourself strongly enough and you have a focused purpose; you can succeed when people around you tell you that you will fail. Sometimes they will be the people you consider closest to you. I am grateful to have the opportunity to impart some of the lessons that I have learned, sometimes painfully, to an audience that will hopefully believe in themselves and use this book to start their own path to financial success.

Table of Contents   **Page**

The Preferred Way

Introduction

With the advent of the market downturn of 2008, our investing landscape underwent a change the likes of which hasn't been experienced in over seventy years. This has resulted in more and more investors searching for a new or better way to make investments in financial markets without taking on a roller coaster risk effect. It is the up and down gyrations of the market that shake out many investors, large and small alike. Some of these rattled investors vow never to return to the market, while others sell their investments for a much lower price than they initially paid only to buy the investments back for a higher price. Other investors, looking for an easy way, spend money on newsletters and other materials, many touting a secret way to riches and wealth.

It is not rocket science to figure out that the schemes to make money overnight only work for the people selling you their materials or subscriptions. The ironic part is that the great majority of the people buying into these schemes know better than to buy into them. They are placing hope upon hope. Some are at such a desperate point in their life that they are willing to try most anything, hoping for a lucky roll of the dice. Most have not set goals to be reached over a defined period of time. Those who have set goals have no idea on how they will obtain those goals. They either don't have an investment plan to follow or they abandon their flawed plan when the first sign of trouble appears.

I can speak with authority on this subject. I was one of those investors who followed newsletter gurus without a real plan or goals in place. My investments actually performed OK when the markets were good, but they were terrible when the market inevitably went down.

I am here to tell you that there is no ultimate secret to achieving riches in the market. If there were some type of secret investment formula that had either been lost for decades or had been newly discovered, an institution or individual would have cornered the market by now and everybody else would be broke. Like most things worth obtaining, success in the market will take a little work.

The Preferred Way got its name from when the strategy was first put together. I was thinking that there must be a strategy that would produce income and wealth, while reducing the risks of playing the stock market. This strategy is about developing a steady, predictable way to build long-term wealth and income within a defined time frame. It is not as sexy as investing in high-tech businesses or trading currencies on an international trading platform. While I cannot promise you riches, I can tell you that if you stick with the strategy you will reduce your market risk and achieve above average returns. My seven-figure investment portfolio is based upon this strategy and I sleep soundly at night.

The book is organized in a way that will provide information that is needed by a novice investor as well as that needed by the experienced investor. Although you may have a great deal of experience with financial investments, read through the chapters on defining your goals and developing an investment plan. You need to know the direction in which you are headed (financial goals) and how you are going to get there (an investment plan).

Although the strategy is discussed early on, you need to build an understanding of the types of investments you will make and how these industries operate. Be sure and read about the investment types utilized by the strategy. The strategy may seem simplistic to some, but you don't have to be a rocket scientist to be successful. The goal of the Preferred Way is to provide a way to make money and get a monthly or quarterly dividend paycheck with about half the market risk assumed when investing in the S&P 500 and to do so in a way that is not complicated.

Chapter 1: What Is Preferred Way Investing?

Could you use an extra $1000 or more in monthly dividend income? The Preferred Way is an investing strategy that will show you how to receive a dividend paycheck every month, while taking only one half the risk compared to investing in the stock market's Standard & Poor 500 Index. It can be accomplished in an uncomplicated way.

Our strategy has consistently generated 6% or more in dividend income and has also beaten the S&P 500 in total returns since its inception in 2008. The initial Preferred Way Portfolio returned 8.42% as compared to the S&P 500 return of -37.0% during 2008! The most recent Preferred Way portfolio has delivered 6.01% in dividend and interest income and appreciation of share price by another 6.25% for a total portfolio return of 12.26%. This is great when compared to S&P 500's paltry return of 2.05%. These returns were made with a risk exposure amount of about one-half risk assumed by investing in the S&P 500.

You will learn how to get paid dividends that are double or triple the stingy yields that the banks and other financial institutions pay on their money market and certificate of deposit accounts. We will not use options, hedging schemes, or futures to achieve risk-reduction of the portfolio.

Earning money with dividends is one of the least complicated ways to generate a substantial, long-lasting cash flow. It is important to have a steady flow of dependable cash. Dividend-paying stocks and other income investments simply outperform stocks that do not pay a dividend. This is not just my opinion. Ned Davis

Research compared dividend and non-dividend stocks from 1972 through 2007. They found that the average return of non-dividend stocks was a measly 2.5%, which is less than the rate on current long term Treasury Bills. On the other hand, dividend-paying stocks returned between 8.9% and 10.9% on average every year during that 35 year period. That's up to 4.5 times greater wealth generating power than non-dividend-paying stocks.

In addition to receiving a generous stream of cash on a monthly or quarterly basis, the Preferred Way portfolio is easy to assemble and simple to maintain. The core strategy revolves around a unique buy-and-control strategy. This strategy can be absorbed in a matter of a few hours. You have heard so much about buying and selling stocks and about other financial instruments used to make "big money." The "fast money" traders on CNBC are very good at what they do, but high-frequency trading can be an exhausting and time-consuming process. This frequent trading is a risky strategy that requires you to make trades every day or every week. The pressure of constant buying and selling begets another issue: with what to replace the sold stock? You will need a good accountant or a fairly comprehensive spreadsheet to figure out your gains, losses, and tax basis for each investment. You take the easy way and send your stack of trade statements to your CPA, who, in turn, will charge a handsome fee for completing the task for you.

Our buy, control, and review strategy will provide you with peace of mind knowing that you can depend on a rich cash stream month after month without the headaches and costs of frequent trading. You will be able to sleep soundly at night knowing that your dividends are providing you a paycheck or using the magical power of compounding interest to build wealth for you.

The Preferred Way methodology will make you money using the stocks of companies that provide services that people and our economy must use every day. You know, like electricity, oil, natural gas, water, and the transportation of these products. Chances are that some of these companies and stocks will be familiar to you.

You will be shown how develop your portfolio easily and build it quickly. Conducting due diligence using Preferred Way methods will save you a tremendous amount of time. Yes, checking out potential companies in which to invest will require some effort on your part, but you will not have to spend hours trying to figure out a complicated formula or a frequent stock trading scheme. Most of the information you need is already out there; you just need to know where to look and we will show you where. The concept of Preferred Way investing was initially born out of my desire to generate steady and predictable sources of income. I did not start out to intentionally create an investment strategy. It began one day after reviewing my money market accounts and certificates of deposit. I found that they were earning less than one half of one percent (0.5%) or less. The return of a couple bucks a month on six figure accounts did not make sense to me. I couldn't even buy a cup of coffee with it. I felt angry, seeing just a few measly bucks at the end of the month on my bank statements. I am sure there are more than a few of you out there that also feel this way. I was mad enough to finally do something about it.

Initially, I thought my goals were in conflict. I wanted to make money from the gains on my investments and receive a higher-than-average yield simultaneously. Over time, I noticed that select groups of investments were showing nice gains in addition to providing above-average bank-beating yields. So much for conventional theory! One step at a time, baby steps, actually, I developed financial goals and a strategy to act as my road map and guide. From the initial series of baby steps firm goals were established, an investment plan was put into place, a methodology to evaluate investments was developed, and the Preferred Way strategy of investing was born.

The Preferred Way investment strategy can make you money and lots of it. This is not a get-rich-quick scheme and it will not provide you with results overnight. On the other hand, this is not rocket science.

We will create our income from a select field of dividend-paying investments that exhibit a lower volatility than the Beta average of the S&P 500 companies. Our financial wealth will be preserved by holding a portion in a cash reserve. The cash reserve is maintained to lower your portfolio's volatility and for making opportunistic investments. You will be shown how this is achieved and how to determine the best combination of investments to fit your needs, investments from the Preferred Way universe of investments. It is not a complicated strategy to follow and it is definitely **not** rocket science.

How the Strategy Began

After discovering that I was earning less than one percent on my money market account, I knew that I had to find a new way to increase my monthly income. I was actually earning about one tenth of one percent. Not exactly the type of return than will send the kids to college or help retire existing debts. Like a lot of you who are reading this, I realized that I needed to generate more income as quickly as possible, not years down the road. In the beginning, I was looking to find an investment that would supplement my income on a monthly basis. Preserving my hard-earned cash was also a very important priority.

I began looking for and researching stocks that would pay me more in yield than the banks I dealt with. The stocks would also have to provide an element of safety. I followed up on my research and started buying stocks that fit my simple criteria.

The commonality of the stock purchases that were made was that the companies had strong balance sheets, paid yields of more than five percent (5.0%) at the time, and had low betas compared to the S&P 500. Fortunately, the returns on these stocks were much greater than anticipated. After fine tuning this portfolio of high-yielding, safe stocks for over a year, the Preferred Way investing strategy was formed.

The first Preferred Way portfolio began after I had spent several thousand dollars on gurus, premium stock brokers, and advisory newsletters. I followed the advice of newsletter gurus and brokers for longer than I would like to admit. My portfolio consistently fell short of the returns that were being touted by the gurus. The returns promised in their advertising were very difficult to replicate. It seemed that my portfolio usually lagged behind the guru's portfolio and sometimes this gap was a significant amount.

The announcement of their investments tended to occur before I received their all-important email or cell phone alert announcing the investment pick and the acceptable price range to buy the investment. Sometimes the alert arrived at an inconvenient time or I just missed it altogether because I was busy working on something else or traveling. A lot of investors were able to time their purchase close to when the alert went out, usually resulting in a significantly higher volume and higher pricing for the stock. I actually was able to get to the front of the newsletter recommended "buy line" several times, but more often my purchases came in later than the original recommended buy price.

What I Did About It

After trying to mimic a well-known stock investment newsletter touted by a well-known financial guru's portfolio and coming up short month after month, year after year, I knew that there had to be a less painful way of earning a decent return in the market. I began reevaluating my newsletter guru's portfolio on a stock-by-stock basis.

It became apparent that if I was going to invest my hard-earned money in stocks, then I needed to be paid while waiting for the all-important capital gains to develop. I needed to earn more than the banks were willing to pay me on my money market and certificates of deposit (CD or CDs). I first noticed that certain industries, primarily utilities and energy, produced higher dividends than the CDs and paid on a regular basis. The companies that I focused on also of lower risk than that assumed by the Dow and or S&P 500 markets.

After initial research and investigations, I found the dividends paid to shareholders ranged from three and a half percent to in some cases more than eight and a half percent. Checking these stocks out further, I discovered that, while not the most exciting universe of stocks, these handsome dividends were paid quarter after quarter and, in some cases, month after month.

The dividend payouts of most of the utilities and energy companies I was researching were much higher than those of the banks and most of them had a better credit rating than banks that were offering meager returns in comparison. OK, OK, I know that some of you will call foul because the bank instruments are insured by the Federal Deposit Insurance Corporation (FDIC). The last time I checked my lights, they came on with a flip of the wrist, the gas cook-top fired up, and I was getting messages on my iPhone! Seriously, although an investment in Chevron is not protected by the FDIC, at the time of this writing Chevron had a better credit rating (AA) than Bank of America (A-).

I started a portfolio of hypothetical utility and energy investments and compared them to my growth-oriented newsletter's recommended portfolio. After monitoring the results for almost a year, it was becoming clear to me that the hypothetical portfolio was paying a stream of dividends that was much higher and experienced less volatility when compared to the S&P 500 market.

The newsletter portfolio was at break even and paid much less in dividends. The credit ratings of the newsletter recommendations were much lower than the companies that were to become the foundation of the Preferred Way strategy.

I knew that I was on to something. The utility and energy investments actually performed very well, generating dividends in addition to a nice return on the initial money invested. This was in contrast to several of the newsletter portfolios I was monitoring at the time. It was at this point I decided to shift my portfolio of stocks over to the high-paying utility and energy stocks.

A Strategy Is Born

I was very happy with my decision to shift my portfolio to the utility and energy companies that I had been tracking. Of course, I then faced the reality of the difficult job of selling the stocks out of my newsletter portfolio and buying positions and establishing the new Preferred Way portfolio. This definitely caused me a few sleepless nights, initially.

As the Preferred Way strategy of investing evolved and took form, I studied and pondered many nights over whether to liquidate my holdings all at once and invest the proceeds into my new-found picks. This thought proved to be somewhat troublesome to me. I also knew that the returns on my cash investments from the bank and money markets wouldn't be enough to buy coffee for more than several days.

Being a conservative investor, I decided to follow a Jim Cramer Mad Money strategy of buying into new positions on a gradual basis. I reversed this strategy to liquidate my old portfolio over a period of time when the conditions were favorable for me to sell. The proceeds from buying and selling did not always match up, but, overall, averaging into and out of the market worked well.

Following the plan also made easier the mechanics of deciding when to sell and how much to liquidate from my old portfolio based on facts, logic, and comparative pricing. I did not get the highest selling stock prices or the lowest purchase prices on the new portfolio. All things considered, I did pretty well. Thank you Cramer!

What is the Preferred Way Strategy?

The strategy divides your total investment amount into market segments: stocks, master limited partnerships, preferred stocks, U. S. Treasury Inflation Protected Securities, and cash. We will delve into details and implementation of the strategy later.

The cash portion of the portfolio is equal to 20% of your total investment amount once the strategy has been implemented. Cash, for our purposes, is defined as short term savings, CDs, and/or money market accounts. Note that 20% is the minimum amount of cash to be held at all times, unless extenuating circumstances occur and you really need the cash. A weekend trip to the beach or a round of golf does not qualify as an emergency! The 20% cash holding is in addition to a six-month emergency cash fund that you will establish.

The cash amount may fluctuate to above 30% as you sell stock investments over time, but the level of cash should return to the 20% threshold once replacement stocks are purchased. This cash holding is very important in keeping our market risk exposure to less than the S&P 500 market risk amount. Most importantly, holding this amount of cash will help you emotionally weather down market days or cycles.

Investment Allocations

The Preferred Way portfolio strategy allocates a percentage of the portfolio by class of asset, which includes: investing in Utility and Energy stocks (those which provide a high yield), Master Limited Partnerships (MLP or MLPs), Inflation Protected Treasury bonds (TIPS), and cash or cash equivalents ("cash" used collectively).

18

I will reveal the allocation of each of the investments after you have gotten your financial house in order, developed your financial goals, and have an understanding of each of the investments listed below.

The total portfolio is to be weighted with the following types of investment:

- Utility Stocks

- Energy Stocks

- Telecom Stocks

- Preferred Stocks

- Cash or Cash Equivalents

- Master Limited Partnerships

- Treasury Inflation Protection Bonds

Right about now you are probably thinking along the lines of, "I might know something about utility or energy stocks, but I don't know very much, if anything at all, about MLPs or TIPS."

If you haven't worked the MLP or TIPS income-producing machines, that's OK.

You must understand that most people that have an IRA, 401-K, or a savings account haven't even heard of or recognize a MLP or TIP. Working with these investments will move you to the head of the individual investment pack.

19

It is not complicated as it sounds. You will be provided with an easy-to-understand and solid foundation of how MLPs and TIPS work. These investment types may sound complicated, but the Preferred Way strategy cuts through investment jargon. The result is that the selection of MLPs and TIPS becomes easy with our qualifying process.

Most of the work of analyzing these investments is already done for you, if you know where to look. We will show you where and how to find the information you need to make a great choice. Looking at these investments will become second nature to you after you have finished reading this book.

You are also probably experiencing a queasy feeling in your stomach and self-doubt is creeping in. Do not listen to the voice that tells you that you will fail at this or that this strategy is too complicated. I felt the same way when I started on my journey to a seven-figure portfolio. The plain truth of the matter is that this strategy is not that complicated.

Get rid of the queasy doubt feeling because we are about to begin to understand how each of the above investments function. With knowledge comes power and confidence.

You will be introduced to each of these wealth-building assets and I will discuss the advantages and disadvantages of each and teach you what news items to look for and how to conduct a mini-analysis of each type of asset. I used the word mini-analysis because you will use our six-step qualifying process, plus you will find that most of the work has been done for you. You have to know where to find this information and we will show where to find it.

Do Your Homework – Made Easy

We will discuss and show you how to do your homework. Yes I said homework! You will have to commit some time every week to reviewing the news and looking for significant changes in a company or its market. Now you are thinking, "I already have a job or business that requires me to work full-time." This strategy doesn't take very much time and isn't nearly as hard as it sounds. As you will see later, a lot of the work has been done for us, but we must keep a sharp eye out for discrepancies.

Jim Cramer, of Mad Money fame, has taught us that the talking heads on TV and the brokers speak in a jargon that is created to maintain the aura of difficulty associated with investing on your own. Why do they do this? They need to make money off of trading YOUR money and investments. These guys spend a lot of time strategizing about what their next big product will be so that they can make money off of your money. The only exception to the jargon-speaking heads is Jim Cramer, author and host of Mad Money. By doing homework on master limited partnerships and utility, energy, and telecom stocks, you will learn to feel comfortable with these investments. You must remember that no one will pay as much attention to your money as you do.

You must also remember that smart choices in utility and energy stocks, along with MLPs, will produce more income than bank CDs, money markets, and most of the current bond market. This will be achieved through using Preferred Way techniques, which will produce smart choices of investments for you. The compounding power of accumulated dividends and reinvestment of our dividends cannot be underestimated.

Compounding means that you begin to earn dividend or interest income on and in addition to the dividend and interest income you earned in the previous period (example: monthly, quarterly annually). This results in your money growing at an accelerated rate. Every person on the Forbes 100 Hundred Richest list as well as anyone else can take advantage of the strategy. If Einstein thought that compounding was one of the greatest forces in the universe, then so should we. We will teach you to respect the dividend. We will show you how the power of compounding your dividends will increase your wealth significantly.

Develop Your Goals

We will start out in Chapter 2 by developing an achievable goal. Then, we will get your personal finances organized and develop an investment program using a three-step process. Only after developing your goal and getting organized, will we show you how to follow the Preferred Way investment allocation strategy. Although you will spend time learning our method, this book will save you countless hours agonizing over the appropriate investments for your hard-earned cash.

Follow the Plan

We will then learn to qualify stocks for investment. Then you will be shown how to balance, rebalance and to maintain your dividend-compounding portfolio to achieve maximum income and safety.

The Preferred Way is not about getting rich this week or this month, but over time. It is a plan to follow and the plan will work for you. You must stick with the plan no matter how tempting a hot stock pick may be. Most importantly, you must develop patience in choosing and monitoring your investments. In a few days, you will have grasped the concept and be on your way to producing income and wealth for yourself.

Chapter 2: Financial Goals and Planning

"There is no dignity quite so impressive, and no independence quite so important as living within your means."

– Calvin Coolidge

Establishing Investment Goals

You need to figure out what it is you want to achieve with your financial capital before you can plan for your investment success. This requires you to first establish your goals in order to accomplish an objective. Remember that a Preferred Way investor's goal is to create a dependable income stream while preserving capital and increasing financial wealth. This serves well as an overall goal, but you also need to establish your personal goals and write them down.

Everyone needs to establish investment goals. The process of transforming your goals into a written plan will keep you on track when it comes to making consistently good choices in the financial markets. You will know what it is that your investments are working toward. You will develop a plan to follow rather than giving in to emotions, whether high or low. If successful money managers, such as Warren Buffet, recommend establishing goals and pursuing investments based on written goals and plans, you should do so.

Once you have established your written goals, they become part of your investment policy. As formal as it sounds, when you are tempted to depart from the course you have set, you can reaffirm your goals to yourself and others, reminding yourself that it is your policy to follow the path you have set. Your written goals will eliminate your uncertainty about why you are putting your hard-earned money to work. Written goals will also keep you from having an adverse reaction when the markets begin bouncing around, which they will inevitably do.

Establishing your investment goals isn't complicated. You create your investment goals to reach what you want and then determine how much risk you are willing to undertake. Start with what you want your financial assets to achieve. For some, it may be investing for a retirement income, paying for your children's college education, getting out from under debt, or leaving a legacy for your heirs.

While the primary focus of a Preferred Way investor is to make enough money to achieve the goals that we want for ourselves and our families, being able to sleep comfortably at night without worrying about your investments or the financial markets definitely comes in second.

The process of establishing and planning your goals is well worth the time it will take to come up with the concrete answers you will need for the process. This process will also keep you from becoming overwhelmed with the anxiety that the market will inevitably cause at some point in time.

How Much Will It Take?

What do you want your financial assets to achieve?

You need to ask yourself how much money it will take to realistically achieve these goals. How long will it take? What is the date or dates on which the goals will be met? How do we find the answers to these questions? The numbers at which you will arrive will affect the balance of your planning, so you must take great care to accurately determine these numbers.

These may seem like hard questions on the surface, but when you reduce the questions to a series of small steps, they become easier to answer. It is like when you were faced with writing a one-page report versus writing a term paper in high school. I think you will agree that it is much easier to prepare a one page report. It will help immensely to think of each of the questions as a short report. If you are still having difficulty in arriving at a "final answer", then reduce the questions further, to a subset of your original questions. When the going gets tough, the tough take a series of small steps, baby steps. This approach will help prevent frustration when you are searching for answers and will create a forward momentum to enable you to continue the process.

Think long and hard about these questions. Do some research if need be. The more time spent thinking over these questions and arriving at answers that fit your life, the easier the rest of the process becomes.

Now that you have determined how much money you need and the date or dates by which you want to achieve each goal, it is time to think about how much income and assets you have available to meet the goals that you set. Take a long, hard look at your current and projected income. Like most people, you probably have a good handle on the amount of your gross pay, income deductions, and net pay. Make some calculations on your future earnings potential. For example, ask, "What will my pay look like in ten years if I can earn a three percent increase in income every year?" or "...five percent every other year?"

Next, take a look at your expenses. Determine which expenses you must pay every month, such as mortgage, health insurance, or child care. These are what we will call your fixed expenses. The remaining expenses are known as variable expenses. They are expenses that can be controlled. Typical examples of variable expenses are eating out several times a month, going to the movies, or traveling on the spur of the moment without regard to your budget.

Actually, it may seem to you that we are developing a budget rather than setting our financial goals. We have not even discussed any type of investment at this point. **We are addressing the simple fact that money that you have tomorrow depends on what you spend and invest today.** The money that you put towards this goal today will have a major impact in reaching the financial goals that you set for yourself in the future.

Now apply your income and assets to your goals to see if your current rate of savings is enough. Your goal may be to invest as little as $100 or $10,000 a month. You must make sure that the amount designated to be invested is accurate and realistic. Check your math, then double check it, and finally, as one of my former bosses said, "super-check it" a third time. If the amount to be invested is not spot-on, it will become easier for you to make excuses to deviate from achieving your goal.

If your current savings and financial assets are not enough, do not despair. By knowing your income and expenses, you will then determine what matters most to you. What expenses can you cut back on if need be and how much more could you save as a result of cutting down on your expenses? You must realize that this important exercise is one that needs to be worked out in your mind. Deep in your mind, you must understand how your spending and savings effect what you will be able to do later. This is really important so, once again, how much you spend and save now will affect what you will be able to do later.

By now you have a pretty good handle on the amount you think it will take to reach your goals and the time frame that will be required. In the next chapter, we will show you how to firm up your numbers and arrive precisely at the amount of money you can make available to reach your goals. OK, it's time to get out the notebook, define the cost of your goals, and determine the amount of money that you will need to accomplish each. It's important to write everything down. In your mind, a goal is only a vague hope that things will turn out well. When you transfer your goals from your mind and commit them to paper or pixels, it becomes a goal that can be tested and measured every month, every quarter, and every year.

You Gotta Have A Plan!

"First comes thought; then organization of that thought, into ideas and plans; then transformation of those plans into reality."

– Napoleon Hill

What do you think about a construction company attempting to build a new building without having the architect's blueprints? What about having a surgeon operating on you before finding a diagnosis for the problem? Do either of these ideas sound like a good plan to you? No, I didn't think so! Successful businesses make strategic plans. These plans provide management and associates with a road map to follow so they understand the expectations to be achieved in terms of monthly, quarterly, and annual intervals. The plans are distributed appropriately throughout the company in the form of objectives or goals for each business unit to fulfill.

These plans are monitored and measured continuously by management and their respective operations to ensure that the business' goals are obtained. This is also the case with financial investments. The point of the above questions is that you need a plan that will show you how to reach your financial goals. A successful investment plan will serve as a roadmap to keep you moving along your chosen investment path so that you will arrive at your financial goals on time. By measuring your planned results against the actual results achieved you can ensure that your portfolio is headed in the right direction.

An organized and orderly plan is needed to minimize the amount of risk assumed in exchange for the expected amount of rewards that we hope to realize. The objective of the investment plan is to create an investing framework that will generate long-term wealth and income. This will be generated by your investment portfolio. Your investment portfolio is built by the monthly amount determined in the last chapter. The power of contributing on a monthly basis, combined with the reinvestment of all gains and dividends, will be multiplied by the power of compounding.

Developing an investment plan limits your investment risk exposure, thereby reducing loss potential in a down market. Controlling risk is one of the key factors to becoming a successful investor. It really isn't as difficult as it sounds. You must select the right kinds of investments in the correct proportions to be successful.

Making these decisions will require doing some homework and planning. This process will be much easier after you have an understanding of the types of investments you must make and apply the Preferred Way qualifying process to your stock selections. Most importantly, as Jim Cramer says, use "good horse sense" throughout the process.

Establishing your investment plan at this point has now become an easy task to undertake. You already know how much money you have available to invest every month. The amount of your monthly investment commitment was determined in the last chapter by applying the results of your income and expense budget and using the resulting amount, an amount with which you are comfortable. You have written the results down and know the amount of monthly income that you will have to invest in order to achieve your goals on a monthly and annual basis.

The planning is an easy proposition when you know how much money is going to be required over a determined amount of time. You know the answers because you have made a commitment to a written plan and it is also stored in your mind. Keep focused on your goals and follow your plan. Do not get distracted by those who question your goals and objectives. It is most likely that they haven't taken the time to sit down and figure out what their goals are, much less how they would get there.

When you become tempted to deviate from your monthly investment amount and spend more than budgeted on dining out, traveling or shopping for new clothes, remember the goals that you set and the amount of money it will take to reach them. I'm not saying that you have to live like a hermit, but live within means that will allow you to invest monthly. I know that it may sound like I keep repeating the message. Well, I am. You have to stay the course. Your monthly investment becomes your investment capital over time and with reinvestment and the compounding principle you will be well on your way to reaching your goal.

Creating Your Plan

Creating your investment plan will consist of taking a series of small steps, baby steps. Baby steps are a good thing and are used to keep you from becoming overwhelmed with information. As you move forward in this process remember to keep taking a series of small rational steps and do NOT take any giant emotional leaps. Steady will be the name of this game. If you hit a mental roadblock, only try to finish tenper cent of what you started out to do. If that fails try just doing ten minutes. You will find that if you follow the steps in this manner, each time you take action and work your way through the planning process you will typically finish more than what you originally intended.

1) The first step in creating your investment plan is to subject the goals you created in the previous chapter to a series of reality-check questions as follows: Are my goals realistic and achievable? (Take some extra time to review the goals you wrote down at the end of Chapter 1. Reevaluate the amount of money you determined you would have available for investment on a monthly basis.)How much of my money or assets are available now?

2) Do my income and expenses allow for additional investments on a regular basis?

31

3) Does the plan minimize my market risk?

4) Does my financial and emotional makeup allow me to follow this plan?

You will experience good and bad times in the financial markets, but beware! In good financial times you will be tempted to deviate from your plan.

You probably are thinking, "Write it down, write it down. This all sounds repetitious." You are absolutely right and it is done with the objective of burning your goals and plans into your subconscious mind, so that thinking about them and what it takes to reach them will become second nature to you. When something becomes second nature, it is much easier to deal with. Transforming your written goals into a written investment plan will keep you on track and help you make consistently good choices and adjustments in the financial markets. You will have a plan to follow, rather than giving in to emotions, whether high or low.

If the money managers on Wall Street and in Omaha establish goals and pursue the market based on their goals and plans, you should also. When you have established your written goals, they became part of your investment policy. Your investment plan will serve as the roadmap to achieving your financial goals.

You must realize that this important exercise is one that must be worked out in your mind. Deep in your mind you understand how spending and saving affect what you will be able to do later. At this point, we have not even discussed which financial assets will be our choices for investment. We are addressing the simple fact that the money that you have tomorrow depends on what you spend (or save) today. You must control your spending and budget monthly. After your weekly or monthly expenses, you know how much is left.

If you find that you need to trim your monthly expenses, trim them realistically or you will be setting yourself up for failure. Ask yourself, how much money can I afford to commit to achieve my financial objective? Then ask yourself, how much money am I **willing** to commit each month? Remember that by compounding your investment, it will grow faster when it is reinvested and when you make additional contributions on a regular basis. We are now on our way to determining the amount of money and size of portfolio that will be needed. It doesn't matter whether you start with $100 or $100,000, the Preferred Way strategy can work for you when you continue over time and take advantage of the power of compounding your investments.

There are many free financial calculators on the internet. These calculators will tell you how much money you will need in order to reach your goals. They will also tell you how much you need to save each month and how long it will be before your money runs out. While none of these calculators will produce the same answer, if they all say that you will be broke at age 65 to 75, then you know that you will either have to work longer, save more money, or spend less during retirement. Unfortunately, some people will have to do all three. Others will reach their goals because they took the time to write them down. They knew what actions needed to be taken and could measure their results with financial calculators. Most importantly, they won the battle of the mind by establishing written goals instead of following a vague plan.

Begin by inputting your information into whatever financial calculator you feel is the best one to meet your needs. After looking over the results from your financial calculator, compare them to the results of the financial goals you established. How did the financial calculator results compare to your goals? If you are close, then great! If not, then you need to revisit how you can increase your income and savings, decrease your expenses, or do some combination of the two.

Be sure to double-check your work. You may have to make an adjustment to these calculations periodically, which is perfectly fine, but do not fall into the habit of continuously grinding out numbers. Grinding out numbers two or three times a day will become a chore and most people don't like doing chores. Besides, continuously making calculations is not a great use of your most valuable resource – your time.

Emotional Protection

I know that this sounds a little off the beaten path, but you have to follow this advice.

We must protect ourselves from ourselves! What does this mean? It means we must have an organized investment plan in order to protect our assets from our emotions. Humans naturally seek approval and acceptance from our fellow humans and, as such, we are subject to swings in our emotional state, fads, and manias. Conformity is widely recognized as the path of least resistance, which makes it easy to fall into a herd mentality. Nothing against humans; it's just the way we are wired. When Wall Street is surging and the financial media is full of rosy predictions, it is easy and comfortable to get on board and, thus, become a part of the herd. When the financial media portrays gloom and uncertainty, it is very tempting to sell at the bottom of a market downturn.

How can you avoid the temptation to join the herd when big market swings occur? You could avoid listening to the daily news or may be even move to an isolated island or remote town. It is by design that one of the best all-time investors in the world, Warren Buffett, maintains his headquarters in Omaha, Nebraska, far away from the financial capital of the United States, New York City. It is not a coincidence! By remaining in his Omaha office, Mr. Buffett is not subjected to the everyday whims of Wall Street. So what are you supposed to do? Well, no one realistically expects to move just to achieve isolation so that they won't become distracted. Armed with an investment plan, you can limit the amount of time you spend following the market and listening to the pundits. We will cover the pundits, what they do and why they do it, a little later. You will find it very amusing.

Stay the Course

Now we will establish your financial investment plan. The objective of establishing your investment plan is to create a successful framework for structuring your portfolio in such a manner that the goals that have been established will be reached.

Why and how will this work? If you do a good job in setting up your investment plan, then you will have a greater likelihood of knowing what will happen to your investment plan as the market shifts over time. You may not be able to predict your exact returns in an up or down market, but you will have a good idea of the trend of the market. You will be able to forecast the stock market's impact on your portfolio as a result of a decline in the market. Being able to gauge the market impact on your holdings will bring you peace of mind in difficult times. If and when the bad years do occur and your portfolio suffers a loss, you won't be surprised or shocked. You must have a plan in place to deal with these gut-wrenching declines.

What about when the market is good? Well, your plan will also help you maintain discipline in up markets. This will help you avoid investment products that are developed by the sellers of high-risk, high-return investment schemes during up markets. Institutions and their brokers come out with new products during up markets in order to attract more investors' capital. At the very least your investment plan will keep you away from stock offerings that promise high returns and have yet to produce any revenue.

If you feel enticed by your broker, you should heed some great advice by Robert J. Ringer. Mr. Ringer suggested that if you want to lock in a guaranteed 20% or higher return on your money, go to the store and buy sales items in bulk quantities. That advice has served me well over several decades. It will also save you a ton of money in the long run. Most importantly, it keeps the money in your pocket and not in someone else's. If someone calls you with an offer of an enticing return in which to invest, let's say an emerging market widget company, think of your goals and investment policy then politely say goodbye and hang up.

With your written investment plan completed and in hand, you will be able to act rationally, not emotionally. With an investment plan that is paying you an income through good and bad financial times, you will be less inclined to panic and sell at the market low point while the financial herd takes their money out of the market and gallops off into the financial unknown. We know that large declines can and do happen. Does anybody remember 2008? Many individual and institutional investors panicked and sold their stock portfolios. Those sellers who did not reinvest in the stock market missed a nice recovery.

The point is that a well thought out investment plan removes the emotional decisions and will prevent you from making a huge mistake in selling into a market low point or falling victim to an investment scheme that "guarantees" a high fixed rate of return while charging high commissions.

Later, you will be shown how to implement your investment plan using a series of small steps. Once again, baby steps are a good thing. As you move forward in this process remember to keep taking a series of small rational steps, which will help you avoid taking giant emotional leaps.

Investing With and Without a Plan

Let's compare our organized approach to investing with the more traditional method used by investors. The typical investor limits their holdings to the trio of stocks, bonds, and money market assets. The amount invested in each is usually the result of a random decision, taken without much thought or attention paid to the needs of the investor. This typical investor profile consists of a few holdings that are usually selected without any research or thought out into an organized set of criteria. The stocks may have been purchased because of a hot tip or enticing story told by a salesperson. This investor does not know how to measure the risk that they are undertaking or in which direction the portfolio is headed. If they are lucky, then a satisfactory return will be realized and if they are really lucky, then they will avoid a financial disaster of major proportions.

In comparison, if you follow the recommendations in this book, then you should enjoy a stable stream of income and a satisfactory return.

Remember the story about the tortoise and the hare? A Preferred Way portfolio will provide you with more money over the long run and you will be able to sleep at night rather than experience anxiety over market conditions. The principle of compounding over a period of time will be a tremendous boost to your return on investment, thereby generating even more income and increasing your net worth. You now have established your goals and have created an investment plan and I bet you think you are ready to begin. Not so fast! Next, you must go through Preferred Way basic training so that you will become a disciplined investor.

Chapter 3: Preferred Way Basic Training

Welcome to boot camp! Well, it isn't as tough as the Army and not even close to the rugged Marine boot camp experience. It's basic training in the Preferred Way investing strategy. You need to read and understand the principles behind what makes the Preferred Way investing work so that you can make it work for you. It is working for me today, just as it did during the market's dark days during 2008. During that year I learned what sticking with your strategy really means. There is no pot of gold at the end of the rainbow, but I live very comfortably in early retirement without concern about financial issues. You can do this too.

In order to obtain success in the financial markets, you need to learn what has worked well, why it has worked, and why it will continue to work on a steady basis. Learning how these investments work over time will help you gain an advantage in the market. Enough emphasis cannot be placed on the how and the what. You will also learn about the when. Learning the principles of the strategy will propel you towards your financial objectives.

Do not be influenced by various promises of making money in the market fast or getting rich overnight by using a new strategy or newly discovered market secret. These people want to separate you from your hard-earned money by selling you one of their skillfully crafted marketing schemes. The only guaranteed return that you can receive without a hassle is to buy things on sale. Buying on sale will usually result in a savings of 5% to 25% or more. You are here to produce income and make money, not to be separated from it by a smooth promoter.

The Preferred Way investing principles and techniques work and are tried and true axioms of investing. These are principles and techniques that have been used by many well-known and successful investors in past and present economic market conditions. You may have heard of some of these principles previously, but take your time and read through this list of principles that must be adhered to.

Preferred Way Principles

Keep It Simple

You will invest in financial assets that are needed by most people on a daily basis. These investments will pay you a handsome dividend while you work towards achieving your goal of increasing your personal wealth, while at the same time protecting your capital as much as possible. We always want to be paid while we hold Preferred Way investments. All the other stuff, like hedge funds, options, and CD-linked futures, will leave you wiser, but most likely poorer. We will cover the types of assets in which you will invest later in the book.

Do Your Homework

Completing your homework in a timely manner can have a major effect on the success of your investment returns. Said another way, if you do your homework on time, then you will increase your chances of making more money. Depending on the timing, you can, in some cases, make a lot more money. This should be motivation while you are doing your homework. The alternative is not completing your homework on time or not doing all of your homework and making an investment when you are not fully armed with the appropriate information. Know your companies' financial positions and keep abreast of developments that could potentially impact your portfolio's performance.

Buy High-Yielding Utility, Energy, and MLP Stocks to Build Long-Term Wealth

When we speak in terms of high yield, we are not referring to high-risk stocks. Following the Preferred Way strategy, you are only taking market risk that is about 50% when compared to the S&P 500 Index market risk. You will be shown how to get paid 5%, 6%, and 7% plus, while you wait for capital gains on companies that provide basic necessities that we need every day, such as lights, water, and oil – you get the picture. Also, keep in mind that over 15-year periods stocks have almost always out-performed bonds and have left bank accounts in the rear view mirror. Sometimes stocks will plunge, but avoiding stocks isn't the answer. Do not rely solely on yield when buying. Yield won't last for long without growth. Owning these high-yield dividend-paying stocks in the right proportion will be of tremendous value, not only financially, but also emotionally, which is something we will discuss in detail later.

Buy TIPS for Inflation Protection

Treasury Inflation-Protected Securities (or TIPS) are the inflation-indexed bonds issued by the U.S. Treasury. The principal is adjusted to the Consumer Price Index (CPI), the most commonly-used measure of inflation. When the CPI rises, the principal amount is adjusted upward. If the index falls, then your principal amount adjusts downwards. The coupon rate is maintained at a constant, but generates a different amount of interest when multiplied by the inflation-adjusted principal, thereby protecting the holder against inflation. TIPS have maturities of 5, 10, and 30 years and are available from the U. S. Treasury electronically.

Maintain a Significant Cash Position

A significant cash position must be held in order to protect you from the volatility of the market. The recommended cash position for this portfolio is to maintain liquidity of between 10% and 20% of your portfolio total. This will act as a buffer on the down days. While a down day in the market is no fun, holding a sizeable amount of cash serves as an emotional buffer. It buffers you from reacting emotionally rather than making a response based on facts and the research that you have done on your investment choices. It is particularly important that you have access to funds on the down days because it is then that buying opportunities are more likely to present themselves. It is much easier to rebalance your portfolio when you buy investments at low prices and later sell only a small piece of your winners or liquidate a position that has grown stale.

Portfolio Diversification

As Jim Cramer continually points out, the only free lunch in the stock market is diversification. The Preferred Way strategy will allocate investment by type so that your investment portfolio's beta is less than the S&P 500 market index. That's right. While we may not follow the current thinking of how portfolio diversification should be achieved, it is a strategy that will leave you with a portfolio that is protected from market volatility. That is to say, during some periods this strategy will lag the market and during other periods it will exceed the market. That is how I achieved a market-beating 17.8% return during 2010 and a 7.4% return during 2011, with 0.52 beta.

Although stocks win the race in the long-term, you and I also live in the short term. You need to generate current income with a low-risk strategy that will also increase our investment capital. You need financial assets that provide a cushion of protection during turbulent times. We are talking about the type of financial assets that will give protection to our capital if, or when, the economy dips again. Later on, you will be given our strategy, one that will show you how to spread your capital over a select universe of investment choices. You will also be shown how to diversify your income sources, those that will provide monthly and quarterly dividend checks made payable to you or your portfolio. Everyone loves to receive a paycheck!

Control Your Risk

That means thinking in advance in order to minimize the consequences of being wrong. A good example would be borrowing money to invest in the market, thinking you will reach your goals earlier based on the theory that the market will keep going up. If you followed this logic, you probably would have been wiped out in 2008 or, at the very least, you would have watched your borrowed-money investments sink to new lows, cutting your capital in half. Good risk managers limit the size of their investments, whether on stocks, bonds, gold, or any other investment. They do this so that they won't be wiped out if the market goes upside down again.

Utilize the Power of Compounding

As you look down this page you may think, "Why are we spending this much time describing this principle?" The concept of compounding is very powerful and is the strongest force in accumulating wealth. Reinvesting your dividends and gains on a periodic basis sets the compound effect into motion. Compounding is proven to increase your portfolio's worth over time. Let's focus on why this is so and how it can work for you.

Check out the two quotes below; these are really smart guys:

"The most powerful force in the universe is compound interest."

– Albert Einstein

"Time is the wonderful friend of business."

– Warren Buffett

If one of the world's greatest mathematicians and the world's best investor have this idea in common. This means that we should pay very close attention to the premise of compounding. We will be exploring this powerful concept and how it can work for you. This simple mathematical concept is the foundation of modern investment theory. It is basically a simple arithmetic calculation that is known as the power of compounding. It may sound like one of the buzzwords you overhear at brokers' or accountants' offices, but this is not just some financial nerd's concept.

When it comes to compounding, this is what you really need to know. Put your money in an investment that delivers a steady dividend and/or gains and reinvest those earnings as you receive them. The accumulative effect of reinvesting your dividends and gains can be amazing over the long term. This is particularly true in tax-deferred accounts, like an IRA or 401-K. The dividends and capital gains in these retirement accounts compound on a tax-free basis and provide you with the full amount of the compounded dividends or capital gains.

The following are examples of how compounding puts your money to work. Read through them and try calculating the compound effect using the financial calculator(s) that you used in your earlier goal planning.

Let's say you have $10,000 and decide to put it into an investment with an 8% annual return. Over the space of the first year, you earn $800 on your investment, giving you a total of $10,800. If you leave those earnings alone, rather than pull them out to spend, the second year would deliver another $862, or 8% on both the original $10,000 and the $800 gain. Your two-year total is $11,662 and climbing.

Compounding produces modest and predictable gains over the first few years. Due to the compounding effect, you will find that the longer you leave your money in, the quicker it grows. Your money in year 20 would've quadrupled to more than $46,563! If you'd invested $20,000, then it would've soared to $93,117!!

The power of compounding also works for cash accounts such as savings accounts, CDs, and money market accounts, but if you adjust the interest rate to 2%, then you give up a lot. Your 20-year return on that $10,000 drops to around $14,835.

This proves to us that the longer you leave your money in your investments and the higher the compounded rate, the larger it will grow. This is why reinvesting dividends and capital gains of stocks is the best long-term investment value. You are probably thinking, "Wait a minute. The stock market is also much more volatile than a savings account." You are correct. However, if given enough time, the risk of loss has been proven to be offset by the general upward momentum of the economy and financial markets. As we will demonstrate later, the

Preferred Way investment strategy will reduce your exposure to the stock market beta by one half or more.

Smart investors know that if you earn reasonable rates of return, then compounding your interest, dividends, or capital gains will work for you and you will become wealthier. Remember the tortoise and hare fable?

Reinvest Dividends and Capital Gains

More on reinvesting. If a stock goes down, then you are automatically lowering your dollar cost per share because you are buying shares at a lower price. If the stock goes up, then you will break even more quickly and you will earn higher profits if the price continues to go up than if you did not reinvest your dividends. If the stock goes up, then you are receiving fewer shares. This is also good, as the average dollar cost does not go up as much. Following the adage "buy low, sell high", you are buying more when the stock is cheaper and less when it's more expensive. All the new shares are coming from your dividend, which means you do not have to invest more of your money to get the power of compounding. Compounding is a very powerful force in growing your portfolio.

Invest Regularly

Pay yourself a portion of each paycheck to invest in your portfolio. Because you have established your goal, you know that you need to stick with your plan in good markets and bad. Bad markets can be great markets for long-term investors because everyone around you is becoming emotional and selling into a bad market. Bad markets are good buys for long-term investors. The only caveat to this principle is if and when Jim Cramer gets on TV and announces to the world to sell.

Remember his market call in 2008? Those who followed his advice, even a month or two later, saved themselves from Jim's "house of pain."

Rebalance Your Investments

Once you have determined your financial goals, you should maintain the allocation for which you planned. Let's say your portfolio goal is 80% stocks. Then the market goes up and your stock holdings increase to 85%. The concept of rebalancing would indicate that you sell some shares of the stocks that pushed your stock holdings to 85% and put that money into each of your other investments or into your cash holding. The objective of portfolio rebalancing is to maintain your portfolio at the levels that you have established.

Rebalance every three months or so by paring back stocks that reach 10% or more of your overall portfolio value. Deploy the proceeds into Preferred Way stocks you don't already own. If your portfolio has lower-yielding securities with large gains, then you should use some of those gains to work in higher-yielding securities. If you have a few positions that have been underperforming in the market, then put them under the microscope to be sure they have what it takes to get you where you want to be this time next year.

Overweighting any particular stock – no matter how solid – leaves you at the risk of unexpected setbacks. You may get lucky, but if things don't turn out quite as well as planned, overweighting can be just as much a wealth-killer as doubling down on a falling stock. Do not let one stock rule your portfolio, no matter how tempting it may be to let it run. Take your profit!

Market Timing

When Tony Soprano said "forget about it", I think he was speaking to Preferred Way investors. You must remember that you are not smarter than the market. About half of the newsletter pundits and TV advisor personalities underperform the market. They are trying to time the market. They are trying to outsmart the market, which on a long-term basis is, at best, a most difficult proposition. If they knew how to time the market, then there would be no market because we would all be following the same advice. And we would all be rich. Keep in mind that over time stocks that rise quickly often experience falls that are much greater than the amount of the rise. Market timing can be a nerve-wracking, exhausting process for most small and large investors. What's the best protection against market drops? Investing regularly, reinvesting dividends, and rebalancing. Avoid trying to time the market.

Stick to Your Investment Goals

One year you will make money and one year you will lose money. You have to remember that time is on your side. Don't let sudden market changes shake you out of the market. With an established investment plan, you will be less tempted to partake in impulse investing or buying on a hot tip. Stick with the plan! In down markets, remember your plan and that investing regularly and reinvesting will allow you to purchase more shares at a lower cost. Change your plan only if your personal circumstances require a change.

Have Patience

The urge to make a quick profit can lead you into some strange investments. The sure-fire investments or overnight secrets to riches are the financial equivalent of trying to hit the lottery. These are terrible odds, especially when you are growing your portfolio on a steady basis. Fear can scare you away, even from sensible choices. A successful investor knows that the economy's growth and the power of compounding investments will win out over the long term.

Types of Investments We Use

You have written your financial goals down, confirmed the calculated results of your investment plan, and double-checked the results. You are probably thinking something along the lines of, "I'm ready to get started now." Not so fast!

Before you can fully commit to your investment plan, you must understand what the investments are and how they work. If you already understand how the investments work, that's great! Just review the fundamentals over the next few chapters to make sure you have a good handle on them and maybe pick up a new point or two. For those of you who have not heard of or used the investment vehicles that are the foundation of the Preferred Way strategy, the following chapters will bring you up to speed. Do not despair or become bogged down. These investments are not hard to understand. Remember that a lot of the information that will be used to evaluate stock-buying opportunities has already been compiled for you. That's right. Most of the heavy lifting has been done and you will be shown how to evaluate the information. But first you must understand the types of businesses in which you will invest.

In the following pages, we have devoted a chapter to each of the Preferred Way asset types: Utility stocks, Energy Stocks, Master Limited Partnerships, Telecom Stocks, Preferred Stocks, and Cash. It is very important that you learn about each of these types of investments before building your portfolio. Even if you are already familiar with each of these investment types, take a little extra time and look over these chapters. If you were planning to build a house, you would need to know exactly how the foundation is laid before you could build. The next chapters will discuss the fundamentals of each type and class of investment. We cannot build a solid income-generating machine until we are familiar with the parts of that machine.

Later on you will be shown how to combine these assets. Combining Preferred Way asset types in the correct portions and taking care in their selection will result in a risk profile that is lower than the general market. It may seem as if I keep repeating this point, but it cannot be emphasized enough. Building your portfolio with this strategy will also achieve your objective of creating a stream of dividends, while protecting capital and increasing financial wealth. But, first things first... Let's now learn about the sectors of the market in which you will invest.

Chapter 4: Dividend-Paying Utility Stocks

In this chapter, we will discuss what a utility is and examine the three categories of utilities that form the cornerstone of the Preferred Way strategy. Why are utility stocks the cornerstone of the Preferred Way portfolio? Utility stocks tend to have less volatility than the overall market stocks and they pay handsome dividends, which can be reinvested add a kick to the compound effect.

Utilities

What is a utility and what makes its stock different? When Preferred Way investors think of the utility industry, they think in terms of electricity, gas, and telecommunication ('telecom") companies. These aren't the most exciting to own and some consider them to be outright boring, which is the point. Preferred Way investors find utilities attractive because of the cash-flow stability and predictable high yields that many of them pay. Stability and high-dividend payments are an extremely powerful combination, especially when compounded.

In this chapter, we will find out what utilities are and why they are such great income-producers. We will also discuss the factors that influence a utility's success and share how to do your homework so you can check them out. As we learned during the financial crisis during 2008, individual companies and even entire sectors can run into problems. So, do your homework. Yes, homework, but the kind of homework that will send a steady dividend paycheck to you for years to come.

Utilities are a category of companies that provide the energy and services necessary to power and heat the buildings in our cities. They provide the infrastructure and expertise that make communications over phone, mobile, and computing networks a taken-for-granted everyday occurrence. As a group, they tend to pay out more than sixty percent of their annual earnings as dividends. Utilities are some of the highest-yielding investments in the entire stock market!

These are capital intensive industries requiring significant amounts of capital to build and maintain their facilities and services. Think of power-generating plants and the infrastructure they require: power lines and pipes that run overhead and under the streets into homes and businesses.

Electric Companies

Electric companies are responsible for the generation, transmission, and distribution of electrical power. Some companies only perform one of these functions, while larger utility companies can carry out all of these functions without going outside the company for additional services. Power generation can involve an assortment of sources, such as coal, natural gas, nuclear, solar, and wind power. Coal is the most utilized fuel source in generating electrical power in the U.S. Currently, due to environmental issues and market force-pricing of natural gas, the popularity of coal is waning.

Electricity is transported from the power plant source via power lines, which form a system of power grids. Some utility companies specialize in the transmission of electricity from the plant to grids throughout its operating territory. These are basically the wires that connect power plants and substations across the country, from which electricity is distributed to homes and businesses. It is estimated that there are about 200,000 miles of power lines in North America. The power line system is aging and will require billions for building new lines in the coming years. In addition, greater amounts will have to be spent on required maintenance and upgrades for the existing power lines, of which more than 70% are at least 25 years old.

The electric utility industry and its markets are subject to the regulations of the Federal Energy Regulatory Commission (FERC). The FERC stands ready to reward the companies that wisely make infrastructure investments in their power and transmission systems, allowing superior rates of return. This translates directly into strong profit margins and dividend growth for those utilities. Many states further regulate the activities of electric companies and set earnings and return-on-earnings parameters. As a result, some companies also seek to operate businesses in unregulated market activities that are not controlled by the State Commissions.

Natural Gas Companies

We think of natural gas companies as providing a service to deliver gas to heat hot water and homes, gas with which to cook, and gas to power many industrial and manufacturing facilities. Natural gas companies sometimes partner or affiliate with electric companies because gas can be used to generate electricity. Many of the natural gas companies are what amounts to regionalized monopolies. Although these companies are subjected to federal, state and even local regulation, they are consistent in producing dividends and profits for their shareholders.

This will be discussed in more detail later in this chapter, which covers the effects of monopolies and regulation on utilities.

Telecom

Telecom can be thought of as a worldwide machine that is strung together by a web of complex networks, telephones, mobile phones, and internet-connected computing devices. This global structure affects nearly all of us at some point during the day. The telecom business allows us the flexibility to communicate with others by phone or internet on a global basis with minimal effort. The telecom companies make all of this happen. Until the past decade, this industry consisted mainly of large national and regional operatives.

Today the growth in the mobile phone segment is replacing the landline business that once was the cash cow of the telecom industry. We are now seeing the internet market replacing voice as a staple business. Our phone calls will continue to be the industry's biggest revenue source, but thanks to advances in data transmission and network technology, this is changing rapidly. The telecom business is now less about voice and increasingly more about data transmission. The phenomenal growth of high speed internet applications for entertainment and business applications is taking place across the globe. The fastest growth is expected to come from voice and data over mobile networks.

Pros of Making Investments in Utility Stocks

Next are some of the major reasons why utilities are good investments. First, utilities are often thought of as regulated monopolies because they have little or no competition in the service areas in which they operate.

The utility and its stakeholders bear the cost and risk of building and maintaining these facilities. The company must carefully measure its revenue plans, which are based not only on its projected cash flow, but also gain approval of appropriate federal and/or state public utility service authorities.

Building power-generating facilities and their accompanying infrastructure requires massive capital investment programs. It is also not economically efficient to have a large number of facilities that either produce power or transport gas to extend their operating service areas into one another's territory.

The large amount of capital investment needed to build and maintain a utility business serves as a huge barrier to entry into the market. Few potential competitors would be willing to commit such large amounts of money without some type of arrangement that would provide an adequate return for them and their shareholders.

There have been efforts made to bring about some type of competition between electrical utilities through deregulation. Private investors have built power facilities known as independent power producers (IPPs), which are usually designated as green or co-generation facilities. These IPPs operate without the benefit of a take-or-pay contract for their power output. These unregulated companies are largely dependent upon tax credits and/or have the ability to generate a small capacity of power at a cost lower than the regulated power company. In many service areas, the regulated power company is required to purchase output from unregulated facilities at the cost the regulated utility avoided. This creates some competition between regulated and unregulated power producers. The scale of capacity generated by these IPPs has achieved a level that would cause a regulated company to consider lowering its expected revenue by reducing its rates or purchasing power from the IPP at the IPP's lower cost.

Utilities operate with predetermined rates; provide highly accurate forecasts of revenue and profitability. The regulating authorities set rates to ensure a reasonable return on equity for power companies and their shareholders. The regulating authorities have to constantly balance the needs of their consumers with the needs of utilities and their stakeholders. The regulators recognize that, although customers need affordable rates, the utility must remain profitable in order to stay in business. To achieve this balance, the regulating authority sets what it considers to be a reasonable profitability level, one that will provide the company and its investors with a sufficient rate of return. The regulators then consider all the company's expenses in order to arrive at a necessary level of sales. The regulating authority then takes into account the size of customer base, average usage and determines the base-rate. The regulator approved base-rate will produce the revenues to offset the expenses and sustain an amount of profitability for the utility.

Utilities hardly ever go out of business or default. Utilities have a large customer base within its service territory. Almost all residents and businesses need to use the services of the utilities. Customers must pay their bills to avoid having a utility company cut off their service. This means that the utilities can count on a steady stream of revenue and cash flow.

These companies typically pay out a large part of their earnings in dividends. Utilities reinvest only a modest amount back into its business because their expenses are calculated in the regulator's formula for determining its profitability. Utilities typically payout as much as 80% of their profits to shareholders. This is because they usually have established a large cash position and are limited by regulators for the potential of a large appreciation in its stock price. The typical return on shareholder equity is usually in the range of 8% to 12%.

Utilities generate a predictable cash flow. Utilities very seldom have to cut dividends because of the reliability of cash flows produced by the customer base. The steady and predictable cash flow produced by utility companies are usually considerable enough to provide dividend increases on a recurring basis. When evaluating their dividend growth, look for a company with a track record of consistently increasing its dividend payouts.

Cons That Could Pull the Plug

Although utilities produce a lot of cash and are almost guaranteed a profit, not all qualify as good investments for the Preferred Way investor. Below are some of the risks on which to keep a sharp eye when evaluating utilities.

External economic factors could influence the demand for the utilities' services. Supply and demand pricing of raw materials such as coal and natural gas could fluctuate outside of the budget parameters established by the utility forecasts. Increased competition within a service area is not high on the threat list, but should be taken into consideration periodically, especially if new technology emerges in the power generation or distribution sides of the business. All of these factors could affect profitability and dividend payments.

Increased regulation is one of the most important issues faced by utilities. Regulators setting the base rate can decide whether utilities will be allowed to pass expenses or investment costs on to the consumer. The utility and its investors bear these costs and they could cut into expected profits. Fewer profits mean smaller dividends. Environmental regulations, whether proposed or enforced by federal and local authorities, can significantly increase the cost of doing business.

Utilities typically carry very large amounts of debt. This is because of the size and nature of a utility's capital projects, such as constructing new generating plants, preserving existing infrastructure, or developing new transmission or transportation networks. These types of capital projects require a lot of money to complete and are the primary cause of a utility's debt load. Large amounts of debt make a company vulnerable to the effects of swings in interest rates. An environment of rising interest rates increases the company's interest expense and borrowing is more expensive than originally anticipated during the budgeting process.

Key Factors to Look For

After reviewing the pros and cons, we need guidelines with which to determine which companies are good investments. So how do you know which utilities are good investments? The following is a list of points to examine when weighing a utility investment for your portfolio.

Dividend Performance

The first item to check is dividend payouts. Make sure that the company has been meeting payout requirements on time and increasing dividends over the last four years without borrowing money to meet the payout requirements. It is important to verify that dividends are increasing and being paid out on a timely basis because receiving and reinvesting dividends is the most important part of a utilities total yield return to an investor. The power of compounding the reinvested dividend amounts can be powerful over several years.

If a company cut its dividends in the last four years, read the news releases to determine the cause. If the miss was due to an increasing debt load, or less than favorable relations with state or federal regulators determine what steps, if any, the utility is taking to improve these two critical areas. If the company has cut or missed its dividend target in the last two years, the company is a candidate to get booted out of the portfolio or avoided as a new investment. Missing a dividend payout will also weigh heavily against a utility's opportunity for share appreciation. If this is the case the utility stock needs to be sold and replaced by a company that has a solid record of dividend growth and offers a potential for share appreciation.

Focused Business

Utilities with deregulated businesses are riskier than pure, regulated utilities. Operations that are not regulated have the potential to distract and move capital away from dividends, thereby hurting investor yields. When you look at the company's earnings, their quarterly or annual report, look for income broken down by separate operating units of the company. These units may be subsidiaries or divisions involved in completely different businesses.

Several years ago a major utility decided to enter the landline phone business by rationalizing that the phone wires would be strung along side existing right of ways, thereby providing a low-cost entry into the phone business. The company did not anticipate the huge shift from landline networks to mobile. It didn't pan out as expected, resulting in a loss hit to the bottom line before shutting the unit down. As a dividend investor, stick with utilities who stick to their knitting. The best choice for Preferred Way investing is a company that conducts its business as a pure utility player.

Regulatory Environment

Some states have tighter regulations, while other states offer a more pro-business environment. There are some states which have a very lenient attitude in letting utilities operate in their territory. They tend to let utilities charge more for their rates and feel that market forces will prevail in keeping consumer rates affordable. This is bad for consumers, but good for shareholders. The regulatory environment for a particular utility can be researched rather easily. Simply type in the words "state regulatory atmosphere", type in the state or states the utility operates in and type the company name into the search engine of your choice. The results should pop right up for your review. If you can't find very many results, go to one of the business websites such as cnbc.com and type the above criteria in.

Deregulation hasn't had the intended effect of creating more competition. Some utilities have used deregulated businesses to take advantage of the consumer by charging the consumer more when their services are in greater demand. This practice leads to higher profits on the unregulated side of the business which is good for shareholders, but not so good for its customers. This action may seem underhanded to customers, but it's within the rules.

Debt Load

Utilities typically maintain significant amounts of debt. Higher levels of debt are required since utilities often have huge infrastructure, plant and property expenses to keep providing high levels of service. Keep in mind that a debt level higher than 60% should be a red flag unless there are extenuating circumstances that can be researched easily. With high amounts of debt, utility profitability can be affected significantly by interest rate movements. Low and falling interest rates provide the best environment for utilities to operate, while an increasing rate environment may detract from its profitability.

Very High Yields

Be suspicious of utilities with yields significantly higher than the sector average. As mentioned earlier, a company may from time to time borrow money to meet dividend payout expectations. This should be a red flag, regardless of how attractive a yield may be. It could also signal a weakness in the utility's business model or be a forward bearish indicator of the company. The utility may also run afoul of the regulating authorities if higher than normal yields are maintained over an extended period.

Chapter 5: Energy Stocks

The major integrated oil and gas companies have the characteristics of good dividend stocks and can also provide an element of growth to your portfolio. They are established and stable companies. The industrialized world depends upon energy companies to produce a variety of petroleum products. Energy companies typically have seasoned management who are experienced in the oil and gas business in addition to having mastered the management universe. The following sections show you pros and cons to consider when making your stock purchases.

The days of cheap oil seem to be over. The use of oil and its derivatives have become ubiquitous in our everyday life. We heat our homes and drive our cars without too much forethought. Most of the major industries need energy to operate and use petroleum based products to do so. During 2008, the price of oil reached $147 a barrel setting off pricing shock waves through both manufacturers and consumers alike. The take away from this experience is that when the price of oil goes up, so does almost everything else. Although the price of oil has fallen since then, it has remained volatile at times and not likely to return to the previous super-low price experienced decades ago. Here are several key reasons for this.

Key Advantages

Oil is a nonrenewable, hydrocarbon-based energy source. As people consume more oil, less is available and the law of supply and demand inherently drives up oil prices.

Worldwide demand is increasing. In the past, we were primarily concerned with American usage. China, India, and other emerging countries are now becoming more industrialized and they require increasingly more oil to fuel their expansion of economic growth.

Major oil producers aren't interested in providing cheap oil. The Organization of the Petroleum Exporting Countries' (OPEC) strategic pricing view is that a reasonable price range to make investing in oil infrastructure attractive is in the $60.00 to $90.00 per barrel range. OPEC's strategy is to support prices in the world market that will provide a sizable profit per barrel, along with the cost associated with the depletion of their oil resources.

Many experts believe in the peak oil theory. Peak oil theory asserts that oil exploration and production is currently nearing its highest levels. Unless it has already occurred, the worldwide forecast is that oil production is expected to reach its maximum level of production sometime during the next decade. The theory assumes that after maximum production of a dwindling natural resource, production will trend downward in an inevitable decline.

Unless demand drops correspondingly, production will increasingly outstrip the current known oil supply, sending prices continually higher. Peak oil isn't a new concept. According to some theorists, the world has already reached the point where supply is now declining. Some experts predict that the world will achieve peak oil in the next decade. As supply decreases and demand increases, oil pricing is destined to rise significantly unless discoveries are made that will provide adequate amounts of alternative energy sources that can serve the same purpose.

Cons

Although energy companies offer some attractive advantages, as mentioned above, they also have some significant negatives to consider. These drawbacks seem to affect the entire industry. All energy companies will experience the effects and pain of an era of oil decline. It is expected that no one company should be hurt by decline of supply more than the others.

Extreme Volatility

Oil in particular and commodities in general can be volatile investments. Think about the swing in oil prices since 2002. From a low of $18 in 2002, the price tripled in less than three years.   During 2008 the price of oil shot up to $148 per barrel, before the worldwide economic slowdown took the price back down to $40 in 2009. During 2011 alone we experienced oil prices of more than $100 on a consistent basis.

Peak oil theory predicts severe shortages in the next decade. Although that may be a good thing for investors, it also has the potential to radically change the industry.

Potential government intervention will become highly likely in an oil supply decline. State-owned oil companies now own most of the world's oil reserves. Unfortunately, this leads to the possibility that governments can turn the taps on and off at any time.

The people in the poorest oil-producing countries aren't terribly happy with the way oil companies have polluted their local environment, nor are they happy with how poorly they have been treated, and protests commonly disrupt the movement of oil supplies. Chevron is currently being sued by the government of Ecuador on behalf of 30,000 Ecuadorian citizens for creating "toxic dump" sites near their homes and farmland. The suit is for $9.0 billion and punitive damages of another $8.0 billion.

Bad Press

The oil industry has been responsible for some of the worst environmental disasters in history, such as the Alaskan and Gulf Coast oil spill incidents. Major oil companies throughout the world have been accused of being a major villain in causing the escalation of global warming. The negativity may reduce demand for the company's stock and drive the stock prices down. This would not be good for investors.

In spite of the above-listed negatives and the price of oil remaining high, oil companies are currently producing record profits. Take a look at the cash position of Exxon. Exxon's cash position exceeds that of most of the big banks. We will position your portfolio to tap into these record energy profits by investing in energy companies.

Chapter 6: Master Limited Partnerships

What is a MLP?

Master Limited Partnerships (MLP or MLPs) are securities that trade like ordinary stocks, but pay much higher dividends. That's because the U.S. government exempts them from income taxes, as long as they pay out to shareholders the lion's share of the cash they generate. This type of investment is catching on fast. Ten years ago only six or seven traded on Wall Street. Today, there are over one hundred, with a combined market cap of some $260 billion. As the price of oil fell sharply in the fall of 2008, MLP stock prices were hit hard, but what many investors failed to recognize is that many MLPs get paid for moving oil and gas through pipelines, so their revenues kept flowing regardless of energy prices.

By utilizing the partnership form of entity, the MLP does not pay taxes on the first 90% of revenues to state and federal taxing authorities. The partnership's tax liability passes directly to the individual partners (investors), based proportionately on their holdings. This is a significant tax benefit for the MLP and provides the MLP with relatively cheap funding costs.

MLP status cannot be claimed by all companies. In order to qualify, a company must receive at least ninety percent of its income from interest, dividends, real estate rents from these or disposition of real property, income and gains from commodities or commodity futures, and/or a gain from activities related to minerals or natural resources. The natural resource category includes crude oil, natural gas, coal, and refined products. We are especially interested in MLPs in the transportation and storage of natural gas and oil, as they have a steady and predictable cash flow and have high rates of dividend payouts when compared to other types of stocks.

A large number of actively-traded shares of MLPs are in the energy business. Energy MLPs that transport products via their pipeline network aren't tied so much to the price of oil and gas like other energy stocks can be. The MLP companies that we will focus on are typically more involved in transporting and storing oil and gas products. They are less affected by fluctuations in the price of crude oil. Companies involved in the transportation and storage business collect fees based on the distance oil and gas products are transported. If storage is required they collect another fee, which is dependent on the length of time the products are stored. They are often compared to toll road operators, given the manner in which they charge and collect their fees.

MLP Investing

The pros and cons of investing in MLPs are addressed below and it will become clear why the pros prevail over the cons. Investors in MLPs are referred to as unit holders because they actually hold units of the partnership as their investment. MLPs are an equity product and as such trade their shares on various stock exchanges. For the sake of simplicity and to avoid confusion we use units and unit holders interchangeably with shares and shareholders throughout the book. The focus will be on energy exploration companies and natural gas pipeline transporters. We will not invest in any real estate MLPs, pending improvement in present market conditions. Today's energy-related MLPs aren't like the energy partnerships of the 1970s and 1980s that were sold as tax shelters and many of which were scams. MLPs today are legitimate investment vehicles that offer real tax savings, steady dividends, and growth potential. Let's examine the advantages and disadvantages of oil and gas MLPs.

MLP Advantages

The MLP business structure favors the kinds of companies that create safe, steady cash flow streams. This is one of the most important characteristics for which a Preferred Way investor is looking.

One of the biggest criticisms of investing in high-paying dividend stocks is that the profits are taxed twice, once at the corporate level and taxed again on the investors' level. The partnership structure eliminates one level. MLPs are similar to mutual funds in that the taxable profits pass through the corporate entity directly to the investors, who are responsible for the taxes. You are probably thinking that you will be stuck paying all the taxes and this can't be all good, but you need to remember that because the MLP doesn't pay taxes, you receive a bigger distribution.

MLP dividends are taxed differently than stock dividends. In exchange for not being charged taxes, most MLPs are mandated to pay out most of their cash flow to investors. In addition to resulting in huge cash payouts, this setup means management has very little discretion on how much to pay out or whether to cut the dividend.

One issue of concern is the small amount of earnings that is available to the MLP for growth and future projects. Ninety percent of gross income must be paid out to preserve its MLP status. After the 90% pay out there is not a lot of cushion to meet expenses and provide contributions to the retained earnings base. Without a strong retained earnings base to provide funding for acquisitions, new projects or capital improvement expenditures, management may be forced to go to the capital markets for additional funding. Well run MLPs accumulate a substantial amount of retained earnings over time and become less dependent upon accessing markets. MLP investors can also take some comfort in the fact that the lenders to MLPs typically can flush out problems in funding less qualified ventures or expenditures.

Aside from producing high yielding dividend payouts, MLPs have demonstrated that they have an appealing opportunity for share price appreciation. MLPs typically manage the growth of the company through developing new projects and making acquisitions of their competitors. In addition, worldwide demand for oil and gas continues to grow and will represent long term growth opportunities for MLPs as developing countries will continue to increase the demand for energy.

Cons of MLP Investing

MLPs equity shareholders are divided into two classes, general partners and limited partners. The general partners are usually the management for the company and maintain control over and run all business functions. Limited partners have little or no voice in the general partner's decision making. As a shareholder you are providing the capital for the company to operate, but have little or no voice in how the capital is used.

Limited partners may receive lower returns on distributions when the general partners mandate an increase in distributions. This is offset by a reduction in distributions and results in a larger decrease of distributions to the general partners.

Limited partner shareholders face the risk of greater liability. While a corporation structure protects its shareholders from liability risk, partnership structures distribute risk among the partners. Typically the general partner will assume all risk for tax and legal issues that may arise. Limited partners do have a proportionate amount of limited liability in that creditors can demand return of cash distributions made to the unit holders, if the liability in question arose before the distribution was paid, such as management fraud. If the general partner and management of the company commit a fraudulent act, the creditors may attempt to recover distributions paid to the shareholders for the periods in which the fraud by management occurred. This is known as a "claw back" because the creditors are attempting to claw back the monies paid previously to the shareholders.

Taxes to be paid are distributed proportionately to each shareholder and each shareholder must pay the income taxes on their portion. This can be a potential problem. MLPs will send out a K-1 instead of a dividend reporting form. It can be tedious to fill in all the blank associated with a partnership return, but is easily handled in tax programs like TurboTax. This little bit of extra work can bring large returns, because most people will not take the time to learn about MLPs as you have. They are just creating more room for you on the MLP investment playing field.

The oil extraction business probably has the most risk of any of the energy businesses. There are several MLPs that have been very successful in this area. On the flip side they are under pressure to identify new reserve areas, procure the right to drill on the land, put in an oil well and erect an oil rig. If their engineers are wrong, they have invested a lot of time and money into the project without anything to show for it. To make matters more complicated, they will have to restore the property to a satisfactory condition for the property owner.

Midstream MLPs

You may see the term "midstream" energy companies or assets. Midstream refers to the business of supplying infrastructure to other businesses including oil extraction companies, processing, transportation and storage facilities for natural resources and thereby have the ability to claim MLP status. Examples of the natural resources that MLP infrastructures support are oil and its derivative products, natural gas and coal.

Pipeline and Storage MLP Business

The transportation and storage MLPs are our favorite MLPs to invest in and this why we will devote an entire section to this important market sector. These businesses are in essence the toll roads for the oil and gas businesses. They collect fees for all products moved through their pipeline and stored in their terminal storage facilities until off loaded. This produces a predictable source of cash flow as the transportation and storage fees collected by the MLPs are not as susceptible to price swings of the energy commodity market.

With steady and predictable cash flows, it is no wonder that the pipeline and storage MLPs are the most popular among investors. These MLPs have networks of pipeline and storage developed to transport oil or gas to most processing facilities. These MLPs offer investors several distinctive benefits. Next we will examine some of the keys to consider when contemplating an investment in the oil or gas pipeline MLP business.

71

Advantages of Pipeline Investing

Pipeline companies, much like electric and water companies operate within the framework of what amounts to a legalized monopoly. The cost of transporting oil or gas is much lower than other choices such as by truck or railroad. There is little competition among the pipelines themselves because localized governmental agencies do not award rights for more than one operator within their region. As such, it is tantamount to a legalized regional monopoly.

The volatility associated with the energy markets has little effect on pipeline and storage MLPs. The business model of the pipeline MLP is to collect fees for the volume of oil or gas that they move through their system. These rates are most often negotiated in advance for certain volumes of product to be transported. The pipeline companies protect themselves from inflation and incorporate ample allowances for inflation adjustments. The pipelines also get paid for their committed amount of capacity whether there is product flowing through the pipelines or not.

Pipelines are highly valued assets which have a long service life. Estimates of pipelines useful life are typically 15 to 20 years. Many pipelines are much older than 20 years old. An unfortunate example would be the Enbridge pipeline in Michigan which malfunctioned and caused a major oil spill. The major pipeline MLPs are involved in expanding and maintaining infrastructure projects in order to meet the energy demands of the future. Analysts estimate that each segment of the gas, oil and refined products will need more than $110 billion in the next decade. This amounts to a huge growth opportunity for the MLPs and investors alike.

There will be enormous opportunities with the expansion of the pipeline MLP business for investors.

Pipelines have nominal ongoing maintenance expenses once they are built. The maintenance expense of a pipeline is a fractional portion of a company's cash flow.

Pipeline businesses must have terminal and storage facilities to operate. These facilities are used to store oil and gas products until they are transported. There are several MLPs that are in the storage business only. They produce solid cash flows and high yields by charging short term and long term storage fees. Major pipeline companies usually build or acquire their own storage facilities.

While investing in pipeline MLPs is the safest and most deliberate route to achieving returns that will help make us all wealthier, we cannot ignore the energy production business. Energy MLPs that the Preferred Way investor evaluates for investment will have the characteristic of buying assets that have proven long lived oil and/or gas reserves. This is necessary to ensure that steady cash flows can be expected over the estimated life or term of the reserves. Some of these MLPs will utilize a hedging strategy to sell their oil production for a price certain for delivery at a specific point in time. This helps insulate the company from the volatility of market swings in the oil and gas markets. While this is a proven strategy to smooth out cash flow lumpiness for the energy production companies, the strategy takes on more risk than similar strategies utilized by the pipeline companies.

Evaluating MLP Stocks for Investment

When you begin your due diligence in learning about the financial condition of the MLP, you will find that the criteria you would apply to high yielding utility stock are not appropriate measures to apply in evaluating a MLP. We need to focus on several more factors in addition to those discussed earlier. Listed below are criteria to be applied to MLPs under regulatory changes, if any need to be identified early on. The latter can be accomplished by conducting a Google search.

Coverage Ratio

The distribution of cash flow divided by amount of dividend payout total should result in a number greater than 1.0. If the coverage ratio is below 1.0 the MLP may have to borrow or convert assets to maintain its dividend payout. If the MLP fails to maintain its dividend payout yield, investors may sell shares and drive the share price down. If the coverage ratio is greater than 1.25, this is an indication that a surplus is available for management to increase dividend payouts, which could drive the share price higher.

Debt Load

The debt structure of a MLP should not exceed 50% of its total capital structure. Debt levels more than 50% can lead to shortfalls in cash flow and the payout ratio.

Changes in Tax Laws

There has been discussion of changing the taxation for MLPs. Monitor the news to make sure there aren't any proposals on the table that could serve as a detriment to your investment.

Changes in Regulatory Structure

Be aware of the regulatory environment the company operates in. Tighter regulation policies may negatively impact profits and distributions to shareholders.

MLP Taxation

Since MLPs are structured as partnerships and not corporations, the MLP avoids paying taxes on its distributions to shareholders. These distributions are paid on proportionate basis for each unit or share held by the shareholders. The MLP does not pay any taxes on the distribution. The individual shareholder that receives a distribution then must file to pay taxes on the distribution received. This method of distributing payouts can lead to difficult tax calculations by the individual.

There are several components of a MLP distribution, one of which is dividends. Dividends will be taxed at your personal rate of income tax and is not eligible for the regular stock dividend tax rate. A portion of the dividend may also include long term capital gains which do get a lower tax rate. This sounds complicated on the surface, but all of this information is provided to you and the IRS by the MLP. A tax program such as TurboTax handles these issues and performs the calculations for you. It is simply a process of entering numbers on the screen. Remember as a result of this tax structure the MLP is able to payout larger dividends than ordinary stocks. A lot of people will look at this and not want to get involved with an investment of this type. You trade off spending a few more minutes on your tax returns in exchange for receiving a huge dividend. Sounds like time well spent!

The other component of income distributed by a partnership is an item called a return of capital (ROC). This is a depreciation allowance that is not taxable when you receive it. It can be much larger than your dividend you receive via a distribution for a quarter. That is the good news. This depreciation allowance is used to reduce the tax basis of the shares that are held. The basis of the shares that are held will continue to be reduced until you sell the shares. The key to this is to hold the shares for long periods of time thereby avoiding a tax bill connected with the sale of the shares. If the shares are passed on via your estate, the tax basis is then reset without a taxable consequence to your heir or heirs. This fact should encourage investment in only the very best of MLPs with long, readily identifiable track records.

By now you have probably thought about investing in MLPs for your tax deferred IRA account. You know that the IRS always wants its due and sometimes what seems to be even more. The IRS has set a limit of $10,000.00 for taxable income distributed by partnerships. In other words if you had invested $125,000.00 in MLPs which yielded 8.0% in aggregate, you would have a problem on the first dollar over the $10,000.00 limit. For some of you, no problems, for others, just don't do it! When you are making money, it's the kind of problems that you like to have.

Chapter 7: The Telecommunications Industry

We used to refer to the telecommunications ("telecom") business as the telephone company. Changes began with the Telecommunications Act of 1996 which performed a complete overhaul of the Communications Act of 1934. The result of the overhaul in the archaic 62 year old law was that it generated a phenomenal amount of innovation. This boom in telecom innovation led to explosive growth of cellphones, smart phones, tablets, the internet, cable, broadband and fiber optic.

Looking at the Advantages of Investing in Telecom

Despite the competition, the telecom business is experiencing enormous growth as more and more people use their services. Many telecom companies offer high yield dividends and also provide an opportunity for growth. Telecom companies create steady revenue streams by locking in their subscribers with contracts for multiple years. The monthly rates of these multi-year contracts allow telecoms the ability to forecast earnings with uncanny accuracy.

Recognizing the Risk

The rapid pace of technology change and increasing rivalry among an array of competitors, some old, some new, has introduced new levels of risk not seen before by investors. Evaluating telecom investments today require more research into the company's business model and financials than years ago, when nearly every regional telephone company was a good investment.

A valid question today is "What is a telecom company? or What parameters define a telecom company?" A lot of different business models use the modern day telecom infrastructure and as a result it has become much harder to pin down exactly what a telecom company is. The legacy landline phone companies are definite telecom companies!

What becomes somewhat confusing is the fact that today's wireless carriers, mobile carriers and cable companies all leverage off of the infrastructure created by the original landline companies to some extent. This has definitely caused a blurring of the lines of what is and what is not a telecom company.

Traditional landline telephone companies were not willing to sit back and not respond to the new competitive threats of the newer players. This changed the essential nature of a classic landline phone company. Landline phone companies now offer an ever expanding array of bundled packages. By combining landlines with wireless services such as cellphones, internet and digital TV they have been able to slow the defection of customers from their core market base.

More and more consumers are dumping their home landline telephone and replacing them with wireless cellphones. The wireless phone companies have steadily chipped away at the landline telephone business. Using their mobile or smartphones, consumers are now able to browse the internet and tune in and watch TV programming. Wireless companies now offer an expanding amount of services and in the process take a large portion of advertising dollars that used to go to other industries.

Cable companies have also jumped into these new markets. Cable companies now offer phone services, security systems, high definition TV programming and use broadband internet to send data over their high speed infrastructure and networks.

Evaluating Telecom Risk

Although the telecom industry has lots of good companies for Preferred Way investors to consider, the sector is not free of risk. Prior to investing consider that telecom stock pricing reflects intense competition. Companies can offer noticeable differences in service, such as the quality of calls and faster speed of networks for the most part. Telecom companies offer nearly the same services which mean that price is often the determining factor as to which company a consumer chooses for service.

A company in the telecom market needs forward thinking combined with innovation to keep up with its peers. If the company fails to keep up, it will probably not survive. Today's cellphones and smartphones feature some of the most sophisticated technology available today. They not only provide a way to communicate by voice, but have become mobile entertainment systems and even status symbols. Most customers want access to these state of the art products and systems. The telecom business recognizes their customers as subscribers. They are called subscribers because they sign up for service for a fixed period of time. In general, the more subscribers a company has, the greater the likelihood of strong profits. If a telecom company can't provide a high level of service and the latest high tech devices, customers will migrate very quickly to the company that can provide the service level and devices they require. A company in the telecom space must expend large amounts of capital to enhance new product delivery and continual improvement of service to their customers. This in return requires more cash generated by the growth of the subscriber base.

In addition to providing services and devices at a high level of quality, the telecom companies are subject to regulation by the Federal Communications Commission (FCC). If the FCC doesn't like a telecom company proposal, it doesn't happen. Regulations can be a huge challenge to this industry. The telecom sector is not as heavily regulated as in years past, but is still subject to a series of federal regulations. The United States government has a vested interest in making sure the telecom industry remains healthy and competitive. The FCC has to approve all big mergers and acquisitions in the industry.

Like any other utility, it has to deal with emerging new types of competition. Emerging technologies have enhanced performance and quality of data delivery. A prime example of this is delivery of voice, data and internet services over fiber optic networks.

Measuring Up Telecom Companies

Several factors need to be addressed so that a company's ability to keep and acquire new customers and generate revenue from these customers through offering a variety of services that can be accurately gauged. You won't have to get out a calculator, pad and paper to figure out the following ways to size up a telecom as a potential investment. The work is already done for you in the annual report, the10-K, or quarterly report, the 10-Q. In addition there is analysis completed for you on Yahoo Finance, if you don't want to or don't have time read through the annual or quarterly reports. You do need to know what goes in to arriving at these key elements of analysis.

A key factor is known as the churn rate which measures the percentage of subscribers who cancel their services over a fixed period of time. An example of the churn rate is if a company has 1000 subscribers and 50 of them canceled their service, the churn rate would be 5%.

Another key factor is to look at the free cash flow. You want to see free cash flow large enough to cover both the interest payments and the dividend payouts. Telecom stocks that do not pass these two simple rules should be avoided. Once again, you will discover that this work has already been done for you on Yahoo Finance, but you need to know what the terms represent and what the numbers mean. Free cash flow measures the amount of money that is moving in and out of a company. If you were to calculate free cash flow you would take the net amount of cash produced by the ongoing operating activities of a company minus all of the company's capital expenditures.

Expressed another way it would look like: net operating cash – capital expenditures = free cash flow. If a company has a negative free cash flow, it means that the company may have trouble servicing its debt load and or making its dividend payments. We are especially interested in the latter. If a company has a negative free cash flow stop, do not pass go no matter how highly touted the company may be. If the company has a positive free cash flow, you should next see if the company can make its interest payments on its outstanding debt and payout its dividends. Once again the work is already compiled for you, but this is how they work.

The interest ratio measures the company's ability to pay; you guessed it, its interest on its outstanding debt load. The free cash flow should be at least two times (2x) the interest payments. If the ratio falls to less than one times (1x) coverage, the company isn't generating enough cash to cover its interest payments, not a good thing for an investor. A free cash flow of less than 2x may indicate that dividend stability and your dividend payment may be in jeopardy.

The payout ratio is the total amount of payable dividends per share divided by the earnings per share. For the telecom industry, a payout ratio below 60% is ideal because the company still needs to reinvest profits in building and maintain infrastructure in order to remain competitive. If the payout ratio exceeds 75%, be careful because it indicates the company will most likely have to take on more debt or raise more capital to finance their ventures.

Why We Like Telecom Stocks

Consumers are using unprecedented amounts of voice, text and video streaming services. The demand curve for these services is expected to continue rapid expansion over the next decade. Currently telecoms have massive capital expansion programs under way and will continue building out more advanced networks, laying more fiber optic cable and enhanced satellite transmission to keep pace. Businesses are now dependent upon data services as their work forces communicate with their clients via office PCs, smartphones or tablets whether from their office or out in the field. This continued demand for voice and data services by businesses and their customers will require more power to be generated and transmitted by electric utilities which creates a winning demand combination situation for Preferred Way investors.

The Preferred Way

Chapter 8: Preferred Stocks

It is fair to say that, as an investment type, preferred stocks are misunderstood by a lot of the investing public. There is not a lot of discussion about them on the business channels and you will have to dig deep into the Wall Street Journal to find information about preferred stocks (also known as "preferreds"). They are not the sexy investment that brokers like to tout because the purchasers of preferred stocks tend to hold them for longer than the average common stock-holding period. There is not a lot of commission in clients buying and holding stock for long periods of time.

You need to have a basic understanding of how this investment works. Once you have a fundamental understanding, our approach to investing in this overlooked class of investment will become clear and easy to understand and deal with.

Next is an overview that will cover the nature and the basics of this hybrid stock investment. After the overview, we will then narrow our focus and concentrate on the exact type of preferred shares we are looking to add to the portfolio. The listing of the various types is so that you will have an understanding of the overall preferred stock universe. The type of preferred stock that is used in the Preferred Way investing strategy is a narrow portion of the entire universe of preferred stocks. Before you panic from looking at some of the following types of preferreds, we invest only in preferred stock that has a cumulative dividend and is callable at a par price.

What is a Preferred Stock?

Preferred stocks are sometimes called preferred shares or just preferred. A preferred stock is a special kind of equity (stock) security that has the properties of both a stock and a bond. As a result of this combination of stock and bond characteristics, this class of stock is considered to be a hybrid instrument. Preferred stock shareholders have a claim on the company's assets that is senior or higher in standing than common stock shareholders. While preferred stocks may be senior to common stocks, they are junior or subordinate to bonds in terms of claim or rights to their share of a company's assets. This is very important concerning a number of scenarios, including a credit default or failure of the company to repay its obligations on timely basis. In other words, your preferred stock holding will have priority claim on the assets of a company before common stock holders, but only after the claims of bond holders have been satisfied. You can also think of it as a stock with a credit enhancement.

Preferred stocks pay an attractive dividend rate and will have precedence over common stocks in the payment of dividends. Preferred stocks also have a preference over common stock in a liquidation scenario. Once again, we have the opportunity to get paid our money before the common shareholders. These two attributes are somewhat tempered by the fact that preferreds usually have no voting rights. The provisions of a preferred stock issue may also feature a convertibility clause or section. These provisions along with other stipulations of the preferred stock issued by a company can be found in the "Certificate of Designation".

The major credit rating agencies, like Standard & Poor and Moody's, rate preferred stocks in a similar manner as they rate bonds. The most significant difference being that preferred stocks are typically rated lower than the bonds issued by the same company. This rating differential is largely due to bonds having more substantial guarantees for interest payments and outweighs the preferred shares claim on dividends. Just as preferred stocks will have a priority over the common stock in the event of liquidation, the bonds carry a priority over the preferred in liquidation.

This description of the securities pecking order may sound theoretical to most, but it becomes most important if a default, bankruptcy, or failure to meet certain obligations comes into play. While this investment may not be as safe as a bond, it does have protections to make sure the holders get paid dividends before the common shareholders. Also, as you will see, there is a nice rate of dividend payout combined with an opportunity to realize some growth.

Major Characteristics of Preferred Stocks

It is helpful to think of preferreds as unique category of shares that may have a permutation of features not usually found in common stocks. The following characteristic and traits are found in preferred stocks:

> **1)** Priority in dividends. That is preferred shareholders get paid their dividends before common stock holders.

> **2)** Preference in assets in the event of liquidation.

> **3)** Convertible into common stock.

4) Callable at the option of the corporation.

5) Nonvoting.

Another way to think of the priority of a preferred stockholder's claim versus the common stock claim, is the preferred holder will get paid first. This is also known as holding or having priority or preference. A preference is not a guarantee by a company, but the preferred shareholders must get paid their dividend prior to any common shares receiving a dividend payment.

A preferred stock issue can be deemed to be either cumulative or noncumulative, but not both. A preferred share issue is cumulative if it has provisions that necessitate that if a company does not pay the stated preferred dividend amount or pays any amount less than the stated amount, the company must make it up at some later point. This is known as a passed dividend or passed dividend period. A cumulative preferred share continues to accumulate each time the company declares a passed dividend period. The cumulative dividends not paid to the preferred shareholders as a result of the company not paying the dividends are for accounting purposes said to be in arrears. These dividends in arrears must be paid before a common stock dividend can be paid.

Dividends accumulate with each passed dividend period, which can be quarterly, semi-annually, or annually. When a dividend is not paid on time, it has "passed" and all passed dividends on a cumulative stock is a dividend in arrears. We want to be paid our dividends and not be passed over as may happen to straight preferred and common shareholders.

Important Features of Preferred Stock

Preferred stocks have a "par" value assigned to them which represents in essence a liquidation value. The par value is determined by the amount of capital contribution a company received when the preferred shares went on the market for sale. This represents the amount of capital that was contributed to the corporation when the shares were first issued. As Preferred Way investors, we want to buy cumulative issues when they are trading for less than the stated par value. This assures an upside if the company calls the stock and the stock is not trading for more than the par value when called.

In the event of liquidation the preferred shareholders will have a claim on any of the monies realized from the liquidation. The preferreds' claim on the liquidation proceeds will be in the amount of its stated par value, unless otherwise stipulated. This claim of par value has priority over a common stock claim on the proceeds. The common stock is allowed a residual claim which means they can only receive monies on the remaining amount of proceeds.

A preferred stocks dividend is described as a percent of the par value or can also be specified as a set dollar amount. The dividend is usually specified as a percentage of the par value or as a fixed amount. An example of this would be the AES Corporation 6.75% Series C (ticker symbol AES_C) preferred shares. Some issues of preferred stocks feature variable rates. These rates are linked to and determined by an index that it is pegged to follow. An example of this would be a preferred stock dividend that is indexed to a change in LIBOR over a period of time.

Most of the preferred stocks issued have no voting rights. The most likely way a preferred issue may gain voting rights is if the preferred dividends have been passed on and are in arrears. There may be provisos that allow preferred issues to vote in the case of a previously defined special event such as an merger or acquisition situation.

Each of a series of preferred stock issued represent, in essence, a legal contract negotiated by the company with its investors. Legal contracts may cover almost any type of business scenario. Until this point, we have been discussing the traditional and long held preferred shareholder entitlements. Below we will branch out into some of the different types of preferred that may be encountered in the market.

Types of Preferred Stock

You do not need to study the below types in detail. However, it is to familiarize you with the fact that a company can create any number of types of preferred in various jurisdictions in order to achieve a particular outcome. The main types of preferred stocks that you may see in the market place include:

Prior Preferred Stock

Companies sometimes issue more than one type of preferred stock. Although several issues of preferred may be outstanding at any point in time, only one of the issues is designated as the senior issue with the highest priority or preference. If a company has a cash shortfall and does not have enough money to meet all of its preferred dividend obligations, the company will start at the top of the pecking order and payout the highest priority issue of preferred stock dividend. High priority preferred stocks yield less than the other preferred stocks issued because the highest priority issue also carries less credit risk than the other issues of preferred. As you go down the priority pecking order, you will find higher yields. As an example, if there were four issues of preferred, Series A, Series B, Series C and Series D, Series A would have precedence to be paid dividends before Series B, C and D.

Preference Preferred Stock

In the pecking order behind the company's prior preferred issue is what is known as the company's preference preferred stocks. If there are more than one series of preference preferred stock then all of the issues are organized from the most senior in terms of age of issue to the most junior or the last preference preferred stock that was issued.

Convertible Preferred Stock

Convertible preferred shares are shares that can be exchanged for shares of common stock. The number of common shares that are given in exchange for the preferred shares is a ratio or set number of shares that were included in the preferred share terms by the issuer. The investor is in control of when the exchange will take place. Once the preferred shares are converted into common they cannot be converted back into preferred shares. It is a onetime event.

Cumulative Preferred Stock

If your preferred shares have this feature and the company fails to pay your dividend, the unpaid dividends will accrue until they are paid in full.

Exchangeable Preferred Stock

This feature includes an option which provides the opportunity to exchange preferred shares for other predetermined types of financial instruments if certain specified conditions are fulfilled.

Participating Preferred Stock

This type of preferred shares provides the potential to receive an additional amount of dividends if the company accomplishes certain predetermined financial targets. The shareholders of this class of preferred stock will be paid their dividends along with other types of preferred shares, regardless of how the company performs. This type of dividend is often paid on an annual basis. Examples of financial targets to be achieved would be sales or earnings figures that were established at the time of issue to the investors.

Perpetual Preferred Stock

This class of shares also does not have a fixed date at which shares will be redeemed by the company. The company typically predetermines conditions under which it will be allowed to choose whether to redeem the shares at the company's discretion.

Putable Preferred Stock

This class of preferred allows the shareholder to put the stock to the company or force the company to buy the shares if the predetermined conditions are met. The shareholder takes the initiative in beginning the trade.

Non-cumulative Preferred Stock

This is a type of preferred that Preferred Way investors should avoid. This type of preferred does not provide for the accrual of unpaid dividends. Typically, if the shareholders of this class are not paid when they are supposed to receive dividends, they will not receive a dividend payment for that period. The dividend does not accumulate or accrue like the cumulative class of shares.

Why Companies Issue Preferred Stock

Companies issue preferred stock as an alternative source of acquiring financing. An issuance of preferred is favorable to the company since a preferred stock does not have payment obligations that a bond or loan would require. If a company misses payment on its bond, loan or lease, the company will have to pay penalty rates and risk having an event of default called by the debt holders. With a preferred stock issuance the company can delay or defer dividend payments to sometime in the future without risk of penalty rates or a default being declared. The company has the ability to carry the missed dividend payments until its cash flow picks up to make up the dividend payments in arrears.

Another reason companies issue preferred stock is to avoid a takeover attempt. In the event of a takeover attempt, a series of preferred is issued and do not include specific provisions or liquidation values. The board of directors will determine at the appropriate time the specific terms and conditions along with the liquidation value of this incremental series of preferred. The board then has the ability to create a poison pill by assigning a liquidation value and terms which make the transaction uneconomic to the company attempting the takeover. Another feature is the ability to thwart a hostile takeover by providing super voting powers in the event that a change in control of the company materializes.

Preferred shares are often issued by private companies and companies shortly before becoming publicly traded. It is helpful for these companies to issue preferred to maintain voting or financial control. A company may also issue preferred as a way of providing financing for the company without going to the debt markets. If the firm anticipates that it may need several stages of financing, it will usually issue separate series to address issues from each stage of financing. Each of preferred series may receive different terms and values. This could result in the company having multiple series or classes of preferred to achieve its financing goal without tapping into the capital markets.

There two principle categories of preferred stocks. The regular or straight preferred and the convertible preferred. The straight issue of preferreds pay stated amount of interest to the shareholder on a quarterly, semi-annual or even an annual basis. Convertible issues also receive a stated amount of interest over predetermined periods of time. Convertibles, however, have a feature that allows the shareholder to convert their preferred shares into common stock. There are provisions that dictate when the conversion can take place and how many shares of common stock that will be exchanged for each share of preferred.

Over the years there has been much discussion of the advantages and disadvantages of investing in preferred stock. Some investors reason that with the preferred being a hybrid of equity and debt, it has all the disadvantages while not having the advantages of either. The fact of the matter is that it is a hybrid and as such must be treated as a hybrid. Similar to a bond the preferred dividends are not guaranteed by the company and do not have the potential to participate in dividend growth and capital gains that the common stock shareholders have. A bond also has a greater underlying security interest in a company than the preferred. Finally, the bonds will be paid off on by a date certain. Payment of dividends in arrears and liquidation value are paid when certain conditions are met by the company. Preferred issues can trade above their redemption price and creates an opportunity for investors who bought the preferred below its redemption price to sell their preferred issue. For example, a company's series A 7.0% cumulative preferred has a call price of $50.00 per share. An investor may be interested in buying above the call price because of the 7.0% interest the series A is paying over time will in effect cover the call price. Since the investor is paying a premium over the stated value, the investor will receive what is effectively a lower yield on investment when the dividends are paid. The reverse also holds true, if an investor pays less than the call price or a discount, the investor will receive a yield that is greater than the 7.0% rate. Moral of the examples, buy at a discount and sell at a premium. Stated another way, buy low and sell high!

Which Category of Preferred Stock Do We Buy?

As mentioned earlier, we only buy a narrow portion of the preferred stock universe for our portfolio. We also mentioned that our strategy is to buy a preferred that has the cumulative dividend payment feature and a par value feature. We need to watch for market opportunities in order to buy preferreds below the stated par value. This builds in a gain on the stock in the event the stock is called for par value. Do not pay more than the par value, even if the yield is higher than other comparable preferred issues, as this may create a loss on your investment, no matter if you have collected dividends. You do not want to take a hit in stock price and undo the financial progress you have been patiently trying to achieve. This style of investing will take patience, but it will enable you to harvest gains and avoid losses.

Even when only investing in preferreds that have the cumulative feature, we need to further slim down the number of preferreds that will be evaluated. We will only invest in the preferred stocks of companies in the utility, telecommunications, and energy sectors. The reasoning for this is that we want preferred stocks in companies that have stable balance sheets and throw off the cash flow on a predictable basis so that we can collect our dividends regularly and sleep comfortably at night.

The resource tab in the back of the book lists internet sites and publications to find in-depth information on preferred stocks. These sources will help you track down preferred stocks and determine if their credit rating is acceptable for an investment. In terms of credit ratings, we do not want to invest in any companies that have a credit rating of less than BB+ as rated by S&P. Limit your BB+ exposure to those companies that are on their way to making a well-documented comeback, are taking steps to reduce debt load, and have improved cash flow.

Are you dizzy?

Now that you are probably dizzy from seeing some of the types of preferred stock that may be created in varying business circumstances. We invest in only one type of preferred stock. ***We invest only in preferred stock that has a cumulative dividend and is callable at a par price.***

Chapter 9: Cash and Cash Equivalents

Preferred Way investors need to maintain liquidity. This is a powerful statement that cannot be repeated often enough. Liquidity must be maintained so that you can take advantage of market dips or other stock situations that present a buying opportunity. Most importantly, maintaining an adequate cash position will help you sleep at night when the market is not going your way. Here are some ways to maintain liquidity.

Bury Cash in Backyard or Hide in House

Yes, you can put your cash in an old coffee can, spend time digging a hole, and carefully bury it in the backyard. The biggest risk of this strategy is that the dog may dig it up and think he has found a new chew toy.

Other than potential security breach by the dog or maybe kids, there is a problem with burying your money in a can or even stuffing it in the mattress. The cash you keep in the can will not increase in value over time. It will, in fact, lose value. The reason that it will lose value can be summed up in one word. **Inflation**. Simply put, as prices on food, goods and services increase during an inflationary environment, your dollar is buried in the can and not working to keep up with inflation. It is earning nothing, nada, zero, zilch. Make your money work for you. Your money is not allowed to take a holiday.

Believe it or not, some people continue to store, hide and bury large amounts of cash in and around their homes. Most of the people that practice this method of hanging onto their money, may not literally stuff large and small denominations of cash and coins into their bedroom mattress, but they do find other places to hide their cash. Hopefully, they are using a fireproof security box or safe.

An acquaintance of mine actually had an envelope containing a large amount of cash hidden in his attic. He placed it behind layer insulation beside an attic beam. He advised that as a security precaution he would change the location of the envelope from time to time. I was amazed that he didn't draw a map or write down some type of clue when he changed locations. On one occasion he spent several hours looking between rafters and under insulation before he came to his senses and made a deposit at the bank. Can you imagine returning to the spot where you thought you had placed your cash only to find it was not there!

Don't know about you, but I would be in a full-scale anxiety attack! It's OK to have cash on hand in case of an emergency, but storing large amounts in and around the house is definitely not in the Preferred Way investing guidelines.

Savings Accounts

Putting your money in a savings account is marginally better than burying it in a can in your backyard. Savings accounts do offer liquidity and more security than provided in the back yard. Most savings accounts allow you to make a limited number of withdrawals of your money without penalty. The rate of return is among the least of any liquid choice with more security than provided in the back yard. In the current environment, getting a fifty cent return on $10,000 is not going to buy anything extra at the end of the month. However, you do have access to your cash when the doors of the bank open or you log in to your online savings account. You do get security in that your savings are guaranteed by the FDIC, up to a certain amount.

Money Market Accounts

With a Money Market account you can expect a higher return than you would get from a savings account. Money market accounts have many of the advantages of savings accounts, but not to the same degree. Liquidity is a little better because you can withdraw at any time, usually by writing a check, making an online transfer, or using your ATM card. Your money may be less secure because it may not be federally insured, but you can expect a little higher rate of return. Interest rates pretty much stay in line with either 30 day commercial paper or the fed discount rate. If you are parking your cash in a money market account, then you can consider going with a bank that offers FDIC insurance on your account. For a little more in yield, you could place your cash into a money market account offered by one of the reliable mutual funds, such as Fidelity or Vanguard. I am not aware of these types of funds offering FDIC-insured accounts at this time.

Certificate of Deposit

A Certificate of Deposit (CD or CDs) is a time deposit that is commonly offered to consumers by banks, thrift institutions and credit unions.

CDs are similar to savings accounts in that they are insured and eliminate risk. This is how the colloquialism money-in-the-bank got its start. The FDIC provides deposit insurance for the banks and or by the National Credit Union Administration (NCUA) for credit unions. A CD typically has a fixed interest rate. The CD interest rate you receive is tied to the length of term that you choose. Terms for CDs are usually for 3, 6, 12 months out to 5 years. When the CD matures at the end of term, you are then able to withdraw or reinvest the money without penalty.

Banks and credit unions usually provide higher interest rates for keeping money for a fixed term than they do for accounts that can be withdrawn on demand like a savings account. Some banks may also offer CDs that feature a variable rate. When interest rates are expected to rise many financial institutions offer a CD that has what is known as a bump up feature. The bump up feature allows for an adjustment to the interest rate when the customer chooses. In the past there have been CDs offered to the public that were indexed to almost anything that was measurable such as the bond market index, stock market index and even the commodity index. Preferred Way investors always put their money in the fixed rate or bump up rate.

Here are a few guidelines to remember about interest rates and how they are determined when you are CD shopping. A larger CD amount should receive a higher interest rate, but this is not a rule. You can expect to receive a higher interest rate with a longer term CD. Credit unions and community banks generally offer higher interest rates than large banks. You are more likely to receive a higher CD interest rate on a personal account than a business account

You will find that financial institutions that aren't insured by the FDIC or NCUA will offer higher interest rates. Only buy insured CDs, the small amount of increase in interest rate will be outweighed by the risk of the financial institution not being insured.

In a rising rate economic environment, having your money tied up in longer term CDs may not be appealing because you are unable to access the money for other attractive investment opportunities. The CD ladder strategy is often used in moderating term risk of holding CD investments. The CD ladder strategy is based upon spreading the total investment amount that is available immediately, as well as future contributions, in incremental amounts over short, medium and long term CDs. This strategy ensures that the interest received from the longer term CDs is locked in while providing the option to either renew the shorter term CDs or withdrawing the money to take advantage of attractive investment opportunities.

Savings Bonds

Savings bonds are offered by the United States government and are sold either online or by a bank. While they are not as liquid as Money Market accounts or CDs, they typically offer more yield and you can elect not to pay federal tax on the interest accrued until the bond is sold. Be sure and call your bank before going there to buy a savings bond, as some banks have stopped offering this service. Here are types of savings bonds:

Series EE bonds are the most popular of government backed savings bonds. They are commonly used as gifts, a savings vehicle to finance education and other special events. Series EE savings bonds issued after 05/01/2005 earn a fixed rate of interest. You can easily purchase or find the value of these bonds by going to the treasurydirect.gov website. You will need to establish an account to buy your savings bonds through treasurydirect.gov.

Series EE bonds are sold at a discount to the face value of the bond. When the bond matures, it is then worth its face value along with the interest accumulated during that time. Currently there is a limitation of five thousand dollars of Series EE bond purchases during a one year period.

Individuals, trusts, corporations and several other types of entities can own bonds purchased electronically. An individual must have established a United States residence and be able to provide their social security number. If the individual is a citizen of the U.S. living overseas, the individual must provide record of a U.S. residence, unless they are an employee of the U S. government. Persons under the age of 18 may also own Series EE savings bonds. Minors are often given a savings bond to be used later for educational expenses.

Series HH bonds issuance was discontinued during August 2004. There are a lot of these savings bonds that are outstanding and have not matured. Series HH bonds are non-marketable and pay interest on a semi-annual basis.

Series I bonds feature a variable yield. Similar to the EE series savings bonds, the I bond series are sold at a face amount for a discounted amount. The I series bond has two components which combine to make the total yield paid on the bond. The first component is the fixed rate portion which is established at the time of purchase and will remain unchanged over the life of the bond. The second component is the variable rate portion which is established at the time of purchase and is reset every six months thereafter. The variable rate is based upon the consumer price index. Interest is accumulated monthly on the first day of each month. Series I bonds are a very useful tool to include in the cash portion of your portfolio when inflationary times are expected. You must be aware of early redemption periods of this bond because redeeming the bond prior to maturity could cause a loss interest earned.

Here is an example of how the I bond works. During the period of 2009 to 2011 the fixed portion of the I bond yielded in a range of 3.6%, while the variable rate yielded about 0.74% during the same time period. During deflationary times such as 2009 the negative inflation associated with the Consumer Price Index (CPI) can wipe out the fixed return portion of the bond when the two are combined. However there is a floor of 0% that the bond cannot go below, thereby ensuring the face amount of the I bond will not go below its beginning established amount.

TIPS

Treasury Inflation Protected Securities are most commonly known by their acronym TIPS. TIPS bonds are issued by the U. S. Treasury and are indexed to inflation amounts. Similar to the I series bond, TIPS use the consumer price index as the rate adjustment mechanism. Unlike the I bonds, the principal amount of your bond may rise or fall depending upon whether the CPI rises or falls during that period of time. In other words, if the index rises the principal amount adjusts upward. Conversely when the index falls, the principal amount is adjusted downward. Unlike I bonds, there is no floor to preserve the initial principal amount invested. TIPS are offered with maturities of 5, 10 and 30 years. You can purchase TIPS directly from treasurydirect.gov and save a fee but you must be aware of the difficult tax calculations involved over longer holding periods. As time passes the tax calculations become increasingly more complex with each passing year. It is for this reason you should purchase these bonds through either Vanguard or Fidelity mutual fund families. Either is a good choice. Contact information on these funds is provided in the Resource tab at the end of the book. This is the one time that you shouldn't mind paying a small fee to keep the accounting straight. It is optimal to keep TIPS in your tax deferred account.

Chapter 10: Broker, Broker, and Broker

What always impresses me is how much better the relaxed long term owners of stocks do with their portfolios than the traders do with their switching of inventory. The relaxed investor is usually better informed and more understanding of essential values; he is more patient and less emotional; he pays smaller annual capital gains taxes; he does not incur unnecessary brokerage commissions; and he avoids behaving like Cassius by "thinking too much."

– Lucien O. Hooper, Forbes[1]

The above quote pretty much fits the profile of a Preferred Way investor. In this chapter we will explain various options that you can use to purchase your stocks. You will find that your stock purchases will be made through a registered broker, whether you use an online brokerage service or a live human broker who can offer different levels of service. The exception will be investing directly with companies that offer a Direct Reinvestment Plan or "DRIP." We will address all three of these options and find out which method of moving your money into the stock market is most appropriate for you.

Brokers

Choosing a stock broker (broker) is a good option for you if you feel uncomfortable with the process of buying or selling your stocks on a timely basis. After spending time educating yourself about the types of investments with which you are comfortable, the matter of executing the

---

[1] The Only Investment Guide You'll Ever Need. Andrew Tobias, 2010 edition, Page 177

buy or sell order still may make you feel squeamish. This is natural for a lot of people because of their emotional attachment to their money. All your homework and theory may be lost if you fail to properly execute the trade. You must be able to execute!

You may be asking yourself at this point, "OK, the stock broker is in place to execute my trades, but how do I know that the broker knows what he is doing?" Before a stock broker can go into the investment trading business a good amount of time is spent in training and licensing in order for that person to have a good working knowledge of the markets.

A stock broker is a trained and licensed agent acting on your behalf to purchase or sell stocks or other securities at the pricing that you have agreed upon. The broker charges a fee or a commission is charged for providing this service. In order to become licensed and, therefore, have the ability to represent you in the investment market, the broker undergoes rigorous study and training. The broker is then required to take and pass an exam called the Series 7 in order to demonstrate a certain level of knowledge about stocks and other securities. The National Association of Securities Dealers also known as NASD provides testing and oversees its members through its self-regulatory rules.

A lot of states require brokers to take the Uniform Securities Agents State Law Examination. This is an exam administered by the state in which a prospective broker wishes to operate. The exam covers topics such as ethics, security business background, keeping records and various consumer compliance issues.

Now that we know more about what a broker is, let's talk about what they do and how they earn an income.

Brokers are paid a commission on each stock that they buy or sell, as well as any other financial product they may sell you. A broker earns commissions on each buy or sell stock order and on other financial products that they may sell. The amount of commission that the broker is paid can depend upon several variables including the amount of money you have committed to your account and the frequency in which you or your broker trade in your account.

A broker may want you to provide them with the discretion to act on your behalf if they cannot get in touch with you to recommend a buy, sell, or new position of stock. If you are providing the broker with this form of limited power, you must remain fully aware of what types of trades are occurring in your account.

If you choose to provide the broker with this option, we recommend monitoring the broker's trades on a weekly or bi-weekly basis to make sure that the trades being executed are in sectors in which you have indicated you wish to trade. As an example, if you have advised your broker that you only want to trade in electric utilities and telecom stocks and a manufacturer of construction equipment is purchased for you by the broker, you must take immediate action and let the broker know that this trade is outside the parameters to which you initially agreed.

Another reason for periodically monitoring your account is to make sure that you control the amount of trades occurring. The more trades a broker makes the more money they make. You may not make money on their trades, but remember the broker makes money on each trade. A lot of trades in your account may result in the broker making a sizeable commission, while at the same time you may not make any money or you may even lose money. After reviewing your account, if you feel that this is happening to you, then you must make contact with the broker and let them know that this is not a part of your strategy and to stop this activity or you will move your account to a broker who can follow your directions.

Remember, making contact with your broker does not include leaving phone messages or speaking with assistants. If you cannot maintain direct contact with your broker, it's time to move on to a new broker or brokerage firm. Brokers work very hard to develop new clients and losing clients is not acceptable to their firms. The best client that they have is the one that they already have – you.

A good broker can often provide you with timely recommendations within your approved industries or sectors. You only have so much time to do your homework and, as a result, you may not be aware of other significant opportunities.

 All in all, if you feel that you can't execute and pull the trigger on a buy or sell order, then this option is probably for you. It is a more expensive option than online brokers or DRIPS, but it's much better than not taking action to achieve your goals.

Online Brokers

The power of the internet has made a tremendous impact on investing for the individual small investor. An investor enters information into Yahoo Finance, CNBC.com or Bloomberg.com and receives data instantaneously, data that once took weeks or months to assimilate. Additionally, the latest news is available to help determine whether the company is on the right track or is suffering from the impending doom of a lawsuit. An internet connection along with a PC, IPad, Mac, or any one of a variety of mobile devices not only makes data retrieval quick, but also allows the small investor the ability to make trades at very reasonable rates and very quickly.

Online brokers are sometimes referred to as discount brokers because of the lower trading fees they have compared to the full-service broker, who may be providing advisory services to their clients. If you can make your own decisions and can actually pull the trigger to buy or sell a stock, this is most likely the best choice for you. You will not receive much, if any, advice on what and when to buy or sell. This lack of an outside opinion is more than offset by the lower trading fee schedules and overall administrative expenses. Most online brokers provide a good deal of research as well. You will conduct all of your business online, so make sure you are comfortable with the idea of typing pricing into an electronic order form and executing the buy by clicking the buy button.

Before choosing to invest or trade online, it is important for investors to research the online brokers that they plan to employ in order to assure that they are licensed within their state or provincial jurisdiction. This step will help to protect investors from falling victim to unlawful or illegal securities schemes (e.g. Boiler Room scams). The Federal Government provides practical tips on how to avoid investment scams via their OnGuard Online website. Do not be taken in by phony investing blogs, bulletin boards or newsletters without an established reputation that is verifiable. Criminals often provide inaccurate information or make hot buy now or it's too late type recommendations. They are attempting to either rip you off directly or indirectly through market manipulation scams. If you need information while conducting your research, stick with the trusted sources such as Yahoo Finance or the U. S. Securities and Exchange Commission's data base.

Once you have selected which online broker best suits your needs, you will be provided access to their website which includes the ability to buy and sell various securities electronically, access to research, administrative and tax tools and some type of online bank access. Some online brokers even combine banking with a bill pay service to provide one stop financial shopping. The administrative and tax tools are very important as they provide you with up to date information on your cost basis, net profit or loss on sell orders, real time quotes and up to date news releases. Fidelity in particular offers excellent access to full research analysts' reports, investment screeners to test out investment strategies

Some of the top ranked online brokers include E*Trade, Scottrade, TD Ameritrade and Fidelity. Charles Schwab has evolved from a full service brokerage to discount brokerage and now an online brokerage. Their clients can use the brick and mortar facilities at over 300 locations or use Schwab's brokerage services with its online trading and research platform.

DRIPs

Don't worry about getting wet. A DRIP is not a prank! Dividend reinvestment plans, or DRIP(s), are investment plans offered by a company that allow investors to purchase stock directly from the company. The good news for Preferred Way investors is that most utilities have DRIP programs at no cost to small investors. A good source that does not charge a fee for a list of companies offering a no-cost or low-cost DRIP plan is www.dripinvesting.org

The companies that sponsor DRIPs also reinvest the cash dividends by purchasing additional shares or fractional shares on the dividend payment date on behalf of the investor.

A DRIP is an excellent way to increase the value of your investment. Most DRIPs allow you to buy shares commission-free. Small investors will find DRIPS attractive because the minimum amount of investment required can be as low as $10.00. Also, some DRIPS will sell you their stock at a significant discount compared to the current share price.

DRIPs usually have minimum and maximum dollar amounts that can be invested periodically. Be sure that you understand the minimum and maximum amounts of investment allowed before investing with a DRIP. Also, read the rules under which the DRIP operates. After you have placed a sell order, some DRIPs may not provide your funds for a week and sometimes it can take up to thirty days to receive your money electronically or by mail.

Company-sponsored. Some companies operate their own DRIPS as a way to increase the amount of shareholder equity.   Most of these companies will usually allow you to buy shares from them directly even though you may not own any shares of the company. A few companies may require that you own at least one share or some other nominal share amount. These types of DRIPS are often operated by the investor relations department. Several offer IRA accounts in addition to their regular DRIP plan.

Transfer agent-run. Some companies have decided to outsource the administration of its DRIP plan. These outside parties are referred to as transfer agents. Transfer agents are most often banks and other financial entities that have achieved a significant amount of scale by administering DRIPs for many companies. Transfer agents administer to the DRIP plans at a lower cost than a single company could operate its own plan.

Brokerage-run. Most brokerages offer a dividend reinvestment plan at no additional cost to existing shareholders even when the company may not offer a DRIP plan itself. These plans run by brokers reinvest declared amounts of dividends only without any additional cost and are a good method of acquiring additional small cash purchases. It is the ability to make these small cash purchases that make DRIPs attractive to begin with. Several brokers are listed in the Resources section of the book.

The positive side of having a brokerage run plan is that you will be able to access your invested funds more quickly than with a company run DRIP. Company sponsored DRIPs can have a settlement date of one or two times a month with your sell price being what the stock's last trading price was for that particular day. The brokerage can execute you sell order while you are on the phone or online, pretty close to the market real time dispatch of pricing.

In summary, DRIPS are a great way to begin investing with a small amount of money. With a DRIP plan you also minimize costs on each small purchase by substantially eliminating brokerage fees and commissions. The best DRIPs will allow you to continue making purchases for small amounts while reinvesting your dividends at little or no cost to you. It is a great introduction to the rewards of disciplined regular investing while receiving dividends that are reinvested. This is what the principle of dollar cost averaging and compounding are all about! Invest in great companies that you are planning to hold for the long term.

Chapter 11: Do Your Homework!

You have probably heard this phrase a few times in your life. Well, here it is again! Your mother and seventh-grade teacher both probably implored you to do your homework at some point and you thought, "Do I really have to do homework?!?"

Now that you are in the process of becoming an astute Preferred Way investor, there will be homework. Our homework will be a considerably less challenging feat to accomplish than when you were looking at the small mountain of books that you suffered through in the seventh grade.

Whether you complete your homework on time may affect your investment returns. Spoken another way, if you do your homework on time, then you will increase your chances of making more money – a lot more money. Now that I have your attention, let's get started.

Homework

Our process for selecting investments has been made easier by the fact that we are focusing on dividend-paying utilities, MLPs and cash or cash equivalents, many of which have very good credit ratings and are less volatile than the overall market. Some of you are thinking, what about energy companies? Aren't they subject to more volatility? The answer can be yes, but take a look at the balance sheet cash holdings of Exxon, Chevron or even Linn Energy. Electric, gas, and water utilities, the energy sector consisting of oil and MLP stocks, are the areas where the higher dividend payers are. The companies in the utility sector and the energy sector tend to have very good credit ratings, especially when compared to the market as a whole.

Do not get overwhelmed at this point. There are only a few straightforward questions that we have to answer to figure out if a company within our target sectors is the type of company into which we want to put our money.

Here is what to focus on:

> **1)** What does a company do to make its money?
>
> **2)** How is the stock performing compared to its peers?
>
> **3)** Is the company's balance sheet and cash flow strong?
>
> **4)** Can the company afford to pay the dividend that it says it will pay?
>
> We will address each of these questions from a Preferred Way point of view.

What does a company do to make its money?

By choosing the Preferred Way method of investing we have largely completed the first step of our homework: What does the company do to make money? Just because a company has electric or water in its name, do not assume that it produces electricity or water. As Jim Cramer points out in his book "Mad Money, Watch TV Get Rich", although Boston Chicken appeared to be a fast food chain, it made most of its profits selling financing packages to prospective franchisees. What you thought was a restaurant actually turned out to be a poorly-run bank."[2]

To get started you will need the company's Annual Report, or 10-K, and the latest quarterly report, a 10-Q. You can usually find the annual report and the company's quarterly results on the company's website. The 10-Ks and 10-Qs can be found on the SEC website or numerous other financial websites, such as Yahoo Finance.

Generally, we deal with high-quality companies such as Dominion Power, Duke Energy, or Piedmont Natural Gas. It isn't too hard to figure out how these companies make their money, but we still have to do our homework in this area. By reviewing the income statement in the 10-Q or annual report, we can find out which segments of the company contribute the most income.

The more we know about the company, the greater an understanding we have of how it operates. If there are notes beside the numbers on the income statement, then we have to take a look at them. What does this mean to us? If the income component is significant, then we have to track it down in the section in the back of the report in which management and their accountants provide an explanation. After reading the specific notes that are causing you heartburn, turn to your internet resources and search for the cause or event on which the company is reporting in its note.

At this point you may be saying to yourself, I still don't understand what the note is talking about. If you still haven't developed an idea about the impact the specific note may have, then we must take action. Either go to the company's website or look in the annual report or 10-K for the phone number or email address for the company's investor relations department. If you decide that your question is important enough, pick up the phone and call

[2] Jim Cramer, Mad Money, Watch TV Get Rich, 2006 page 26

the investor relations department number. When you call, be honest. Let them know that you are an investor and ask if they can help you understand what the note implies. I have experienced a great deal of success with this approach and often have learned more than the answer to the question that I was asking.

Do not abuse the goodwill of the investor relations department by calling them on all or even most of the questions that you develop. Use this resource only when you really need it or they will think that you are the little person that called wolf one too many times. We all know how that story ended! The greater the knowledge base we have of the revenue the company is producing and where it is spending its internally-generated income, the easier it will be for us to make a decision that is based upon facts and audited numbers, rather than going with our emotions or relying on TV commentators to guide our decision-making with a sound bite comment. It is your money and your decision to make!

What external factors affect the company's performance?

We must make sure that we stay up-to-date on the news that may affect a company, either positively or negatively. This can be accomplished by tracking your investments through a resource such as Yahoo Finance or Bloomberg.com. Within in the stock tracker is a built-in news component that is continuously up dated. No, we do not want to become news junkies, but we do want to review the breaking news on the company at least once a week. Reviewing the company news will become second nature over time.

When monitoring the news for external factors, pay close attention to company comments or governmental or regulatory body comments. The difference in receiving a rate increase may affect the profitability. If the regulatory agency is making negative comments that may affect the company's revenue or income line, find out what the company is saying to counter these comments. The Investor Relations department or the public relations firm will always issue a comment that diffuses the negative comments made. If not, and the negative comments will impact the revenue and income lines, then it is time to go to your back up investment for the sector. Get them off the bench and into the game as needed, just as a coach would during the big game.

How is the stock performing compared to its peers?

There are a number of sources, such as Google Finance, Yahoo Finance, and Bloomberg can be helpful to you when researching potential companies in which to invest. I like to use Yahoo Finance (not an endorsement) because of the simplicity of its summary page. The Yahoo Finance summary page provides the latest trading information, financial information, what ratings analysts have assigned, and, most importantly, the latest news about the company. Yahoo also provides comparison info as to who the company's competitors are and how they stack up financially compared to each other. A lot of the work is already done for you. You must thoroughly read through the comparison financial information each time and not get into the habit of glancing at summaries and making a decision.

Is the company's balance sheet and cash flow strong?

As a Preferred Way investor, we typically do not like to see more debt than equity on a company's balance sheet. Also, we need to make sure that the company has enough cash on the balance sheet to pay off its debt in a timely manner.

Before we get started, it must be pointed out that, when looking at electric utilities, we must remember that it takes a quite large investment to fund a power-generating plant and to distribute the electricity that it generates from plant to user. Electric utilities have a regulated portion of the business that basically guarantees the power company a payout that will reach the regulated return-on-equity or other such financial metric.

As Jim Cramer says frequently, "We are looking for broken stocks, not broken companies." My interpretation of this is that we look for companies that are undervalued due to market events of which they have no control over. We have seen this time and time again. A news story breaks what is perceived to be bad news for the company, only to find out a week later that the company had already put measures into place to counter the event. Look past the two hour analysts write up when looking for undervalued companies.

Assets are sources of underlying capital that a company owns which can be transformed, at some point in time, to produce income. Financial accounting terms express assets as having the economic viability to generate a positive economic value. In layman terms, assets are the value that can be transformed into cash. For example, cash is on the balance sheet and is readily transferable. On the other hand manufacturing equipment out in the plant may take a while longer to generate cash either through its production capabilities or how much value it brings in sale to a third party. You know, like an auction.

A balance sheet is nothing more than a snapshot of the company's value of assets on any given day. The most important class of assets are assets that are said to be tangible. Which assets can I put my hands on? Cash and inventory are pretty easy to liquidate to provide a company with immediate value. These types of tangible assets are known as current assets. Plant property and equipment may take longer to produce or be liquidated to generate cash. These types of assets are known as fixed assets mainly due to their long operational life and nature.

The second type of assets that a company has on its balance sheet is the intangible asset class. Intangible assets do not have physicality and are non-physical in nature, but they provide the company with some type of advantage in the business world. These types of assets may not readily produce value if sold by the company, but due to the advantage the intangible asset creates in the market place it has a value. Examples of intangible assets are trademarks, goodwill and patents.

Cash Flow

Cash flow is nothing more than a measure of the rate at which cash is moving into and out of a company during a specific period of time. An example of cash flow can be seen as contributors to cash flow, like deposits to the bank and accounts receivable that have been collected. Offsetting the cash flow contributors would be items such as new inventory purchased or new computer equipment purchased, in other words, expenses. Measuring the amount of cash flows that a company generates over a specific period of time also needs to include the notion of velocity. Velocity is the rate at which the cash flow is flowing into and out of the company.

By inputting these variables into a financial model, analysts can then predict if a company is generating enough cash or will it have to borrow money or raise additional equity to meet its cash needs. If the cash flow is greater than what is required to meet the company's ongoing business activities, the company is said to be "cash flowing". A company can also apply an internal rate of return or IRR model utilizing cash flow information to determine what type of return certain activities are generating.

A project's rate-of-return or value is a measurement of the rate that the cash is put into a project and how fast it is returned to the investing company or individual investor. The timing of cash flows into and out of projects is used as inputs to various financial models and formulas, such as internal rate-of-return and net-present-value.

Problems with a Business' Liquidity

One of the hardest concepts to grasp is how can a profitable company fail. The old saying "cash is king" is definitely appropriate when discussing this topic. If a shortage of cash develops, payrolls may not be met, new computers can't be paid for or new inventory required for production can't be paid for. The company may also be heavily dependent upon its lenders to refinance existing debt or to expand its line of credit so that enough cash is available to the company. When a company borrows or expands its credit lines, it is generating new cash, but on a temporary basis. This is known as low quality cash flow.

The term cash flow can be implied or used in a number of different ways. It all depends on the context in which the term is being used. Cash flow also refers to a specific time frame(s) and can be expressed in the future or in the here and now.

There are subclasses of cash flow such as net cash flow, and free cash flow (FCF). As Preferred Way investors we are keenly interested in the FCF. Here's why. FCF is the amount of cash flow that is available for payment of interest and dividends to all stakeholders of the company. For our purposes the stakeholders are the common stock holders, debt holders and preferred stock holders.

We look for companies that generate large amounts of cash for their stakeholders. Even in poor economic times a company with strong FCF can make favorable purchases of competitors or complementary businesses, buy back stock and increase dividend payments. This is why cash flow is so important when evaluating a company. A company with strong cash flow has many options available whereas a company with weak cash flow sees minimal opportunities in the market place. One could argue that cash flow is actually the single largest factor in determining the value of a company.

Can the company afford to pay the dividend that it says it will pay?

We can make a determination of whether a company is able to meet its dividend payout requirement by utilizing the dividend payout ratio. The amount of a company's net income that is available to pay dividends to its shareholders. The way that this is measured is by using the dividend payout ratio. The dividend payout ratio is the total amount of dividends paid annually divided by the diluted earnings. This is further divided by the number of shares to reach a per share basis.

Here is how it works: The XYZ Company made 4 dividend payments of $1.00 each or a total of $4.00 for the year. During the same time frame, the XYZ Company realized net earnings of $50.00 per share. Using the formula of total dividends per share divided by diluted earnings per share, the company's dividend payout ratio was $4.00/$50.00 or 8%. What this tells us is that The XYZ Company paid out 8% of its net income and kept 92% for its own operational needs.

For Preferred Way investors, the dividend payout ratio is a closely-watched financial measure. In our example, the management of the XYZ Company is only paying out $.08 of every dollar that shareholders are investing in the company. Given the amount of profit being generated by XYZ, management could consider giving the shareholders a boost in dividend payments, which makes for happy shareholders.

Although the dividend payout ratio is one of the best tools to help investment evaluation process, you have to look beyond the ratio and determine if all of the money available for dividend payout is being sourced from operations or borrowing. In the past, companies have borrowed money to pay dividends and make their dividend payout and/or cash flows look good and thereby please their shareholders. In the future if you come across an instance of a company borrowing to pay shareholders, be on full alert for other danger signs.

There have been instances in which a company paid out more in dividends that it earned. This can push the dividend payout ratio to more than 100%. This makes the company vulnerable on two levels. The first is that the company is not generating enough profits to plough some of the earnings back into the company to continue to make it and its market presence stronger. On the second level it leaves shareholders with the possibility of a dividend cut. If the shareholders actually receive a dividend cut, it could cause a selloff by the shareholders. This in turn can cause the company's stock price to go down, leaving the company's capitalization in question. Shareholders do not like to be disappointed or take dividend cuts! Even if the company decides to prop the existing dividend up and borrow to pay it and later cuts its dividend, this is perceived as a weakness not only by the shareholders but also the entire market putting even more downward pressure on the company.

Summary

You are probably glazed over by now and concerned about having to do tons of math and reading. Not to worry, the work has been done for you. We just wanted to make sure that you had a basic understanding of how to use the data and tools rather than going with the conclusion that the analyst reached. At least you know what goes into the thinking!

Once you have performed the initial homework, it becomes a matter of keeping up with the cash flow, income, and other factors that may affect the company's performance. You will probably wind up spending about two hours or less per week looking over your stock selections and maintaining your portfolio. Another way to look at this process is to see that you are investing your time to produce income and preserve capital in a way that will help you achieve your goals.

Most investors don't keep tabs on their companies' cash flow. I think that's a mistake. If you take the time to read past the headlines and crack a 10-Q or a public filing, then you will be in a much better position to spot impending misfortune early and improve the odds of finding an underappreciated stock that is in a position to provide you with the best returns.

Most importantly, you should be able to sleep better at night knowing that your stock pick can amply cover its dividend payout.

Chapter 12: Assembling Our Portfolio

Congratulations, you have completed your homework and are now prepared to start assembling your portfolio. Notice I have used the word assemble. By now you have identified a brokerage service and set up your account. You are thinking, "I have completed Preferred Way Basic Training, gotten my personal finances in order, set my financial goals and have completed the stock-selection homework. I am ready to buy all of my investments now." Not so fast! We are investors, not buyers. Investors build their portfolios on a rational and determined basis.

Assemblage

We will assemble our portfolio over time and when market conditions are favorable to our strategy. We will assemble the portfolio brick-by-brick, stock-by-stock, until the portfolio is built. I know this sounds boring, but this method of portfolio construction will prevail. Just ask Cramer! Remember, the strategy calls for us to construct our portfolio over time horizons that are favorable to achieving our income and capital preservation goals. We have spent a lot of time and preparation to get to this point. Now we must do the hard part, exercise patience when constructing your portfolio. So take a deep breath and let's get started assembling the portfolio.

The Two Powerful Rules of Assemblage

The following two sentences are very important and you **must** remember them when making your stock purchases:

> **1)** You will average into the investments by using an increment of not more than five percent (5%) to ten percent (10%) of the total amount of capital you have committed for each of your individual stock investments.

> **2)** You must exercise patience when buying a stock. This can be a difficult rule to follow, but you must be patient until market conditions and pricing are in your favor.

Portfolio Allocation

By now you have set your financial goals and know exactly how much you have available to begin investing today. The allocated percentages are expressed as a percent of the total amount of money you have committed to this portfolio. This is a tried-and-true allocation strategy that has worked successfully in the past and continues to work successfully today. The portfolio allocation is spelled out rather than in a table format because ereaders scramble the contents of tables.

The investments are to be allocated as follows:

- Utility stocks investment amount of forty percent.

- Energy stocks investment amount of ten percent.

- MLPs investment amount of fifteen percent.

- Preferred stock investment amount of ten percent.

- TIPS investment amount of ten percent.

- Cash investment amount of fifteen percent.

- Beta should be close to the weighted industry total averages of 0 .57 or about half of the S&P Beta of 1.0.

Do not be surprised with the amount committed to the utilities sector. Most of the electric and gas companies have an investment-grade rating and more-than-sufficient cash flow to meet capitalization programs and pay dividends to investors safely. Remember, we are going for a low beta portfolio to mitigate volatility. The beta average for the utilities held in the exchange traded fund sponsored by iShares Dow Jones U.S. Utilities Sector Index Fund (IDU) is 0.44. The Vanguard Utility exchange traded fund (VPU) beta is 0.43. Each of these fund's holdings are very similar.

Now, here is why you should not take the easy way out and buy a utility sector ETF. The Vanguard VPU currently holds 85 stocks, which provide an aggregate yield of 3.65% annually. By doing a little, not a lot, of homework (as described, oddly enough, in the Homework section!) you will hold approximately five to ten utility stocks, which will provide a yield greater than that of the IDU or the VPU. From a credit risk prospective, the credit ratings of your stock picks will be higher than the average of the IDU or VPU. The higher credit rating should mitigate the size of your stock picks versus the 85 stocks held in the ETF.

The higher credit rating of your picks will also provide you with the advantage of not having to do as much portfolio maintenance in the future. This is the best of all worlds, investments with high credit ratings, not having to do a lot of heavy lifting maintenance-wise, and getting paid dividends steadily.

The classic regulated utility makes a great income-generating stock because its profits are practically guaranteed. It can be argued that due to government regulations, these companies experience less growth. The limits governments place on profit growth significantly lowers the potential for capital appreciation in utilities stock prices. These companies need another way to give shareholders a return on the equity invested, so they entice investors by promising to pay high yields (through dividends) equal to or above the rate of Treasury bonds.

The same logic and reasoning applies to the Energy sector of your portfolio. The energy sector is not regulated in the returns it can deliver to shareholders. The energy sector can be more volatile, but the companies on which we will focus all pay dividends and have high amounts of cash on their balance sheets.

Hold your MLP picks in a taxable account in order to take advantage of the unique tax benefit that MLPs provide and remember to keep good records. Your broker statements will provide you with all the information that will be required at tax time.

As mentioned previously, consider purchasing TIPS through a mutual fund company such as Vanguard or Fidelity. You could go online and make a direct purchase from the Treasury Department and squeak out a slightly higher return, but the record keeping is complicated so why do we want that chore? Keep TIPS in a tax-deferred account if possible. This will save you a lot of time and calculations during tax season.

Don't bury your cash in the backyard or put it in the freezer! Check with the mutual fund companies or your online broker to see if they offer money market accounts or CDs at more competitive rates than what you can find locally.

Also, inquire as to whether there is an electronic funds transfer or wire transfer available to you at no cost. This feature could help you move funds to your local bank if they begin to offer better rates or you are experiencing extenuating financial circumstances.

The Initial Preferred Way Portfolio

The actual portfolio of Preferred Way investments that I assembled during 2008 is listed for your review. The initial portfolio yield could have been higher but due to the fact that the investments were bought over time in small incremental amounts, the yield was impacted.

The most recent portfolio appears in the next section. This can give you an idea of how much a portfolio can shift. You will also note the constant that core utility and MLP companies' investments have increased over time.

Keep in mind that it took months to build and complete positions in each incremental investment of each category. You must use patience and discipline in building the portfolio and purchase when the opportunity presents itself, even though it often means buying when others are selling. Remember, you cannot outsmart the market, so buy increments of a position and do not purchase all of a position at one time. If you find yourself doubting a planned purchase in the midst of a sell-off, remind yourself to buy when others are fearful and stick to your plan.

The initial portfolio serves as an example to show you what an actual portfolio can look like. Note the low betas of each stock or MLP. This does prove that you can lower your risk profile relative to the market and still get paid nice dividends and have some growth of the underlying investments.

Different time frames will present different economic opportunities and there are opportunities in every market. Buying shares when others are fearful and selling is not for the faint of heart, but I stuck with my plan and kept buying when opportunities presented themselves. The yield of the initial portfolio amounted to 6.35% and had a beta equal to 0.54.

The appreciation in share price of the underlying investments pushed the total return of the initial portfolio to 8.42%.

This 8.42% return may not seem that big of a deal until it is compared to the S&P 500 loss for the year of -37.0%. Yes, -37.0%.

Preferred Way Initial Portfolio

Electric Utility Stocks

Company	Ticker Symbol	Beta	Yield
Dominion	D	0.31	4.8%
Duke Energy	DUK	0.21	5.9%
Southern Co.	SO	0.09	5.1%

Energy Companies

Company	Ticker Symbol	Beta	Yield
Atmos Energy	ATO	0.41	4.8%
Chevron	CVX	0.79	4.0%
Conoco Phillips	COP	0.85	6.2%
Piedmont Nat Gas	PNY	0.32	4.7%
Spectra Energy	SE	0.75	4.8%

MLP Companies

Company	Ticker Symbol	Beta	Yield
Enterprise	EPD	0.72	5.8%
Energy	ETP	0.91	8.5%
Kinder Morgan	KMP	0.51	6.5%
Linn Energy	LINN	0.90	8.8%

Telecom Companies

Company	Ticker Symbol	Beta	Yield
AT&T	T	0.48	6.2%
Verizon	VZ	0.41	5.5%
Windstream	WIN	0.61	8.3%

Preferred Stocks

Company	Ticker Symbol	Beta	Yield
AES Pref C	AES C	0.86	7.2%
El Paso Pref C	EP C	0.29	5.7%
Conn Lt & Power	CNLPL	0.76	7.1%

TIPs

Company	Ticker Symbol	Beta	Yield
Vanguard	VIPSX	0.0	1.08%

Cash Account

	Beta	Yield
Savings Bonds, Series E	0.0	3.5%
Bank of America Savings & CDs	0.0	0.1%

Initial Portfolio Beta = 0.54

Initial Portfolio Yield = 6.35%
Total Return   = 8.42%

Recent Preferred Way Investment Portfolio

The most recent portfolio appears below. When compared to the original portfolio, you will notice that the portfolio composition has shifted in order to add more companies in all segments and especially in the Utility and MLP companies. Most of this was brought about through the reinvestment of dividends, rebalancing and the addition of new positions when market gurus on TV were forecasting a downturn. You will also note a constant of core utility and MLP companies and that investment in these sectors have increased over time.

The yield of the recent portfolio amounted 6.01% and had a beta equal to 0.56. Keep in mind that the 6.01% yield is at a time when treasury and bond markets are nearing all-time lows and market risk has been rising. **The appreciation in share price of the underlying investments pushed the total return of the initial portfolio to 12.26%.** Note that the S&P 500 was only up 2.05% for the same period.

Electric Utility Stocks

Company	Ticker Symbol	Beta	Yield
Atlantic Power	AT	0.24	8.50%
Dominion	D	0.31	4.00%
Duke Energy	DUK	0.21	4.70%
Entergy Corp	ETR	0.46	5.20%
Exelon Corp	EXC	0.48	4.00%
Southern Co	SO	0.09	4.30%

Energy Companies

Company	Ticker Symbol	Beta	Yield
Atmos Energy	ATO	0.49	4.20%
Chevron	CVX	0.97	3.60%
Piedmont Nat Gas	PNY	0.43	4.00%
SCANA Corp	SCG	0.41	4.30%
TransCanada Corp	TRP	0.75	4.10%

MLP Companies

Company	Ticker Symbol	Beta	Yield
Buckeye	BPL	0.48	8.30
Enterprise	EPD	0.72	5.00%
Energy TP	ETP	0.91	7.90%
Kinder Morgan	KMP	0.51	6.0%
Linn Energy	LINE	0.90	7.90%
NuStar Energy	NS	0.79	8.30%

Telecom Companies

Company	Ticker Symbol	Beta	Yield
AT&T	T	0.48	5.30%
Verizon	VZ	0.41	4.90%
Windstream	WIN	0.61	10.5%

Preferred Stocks

Company & Issue	Ticker Symbol	Beta	Yield
AES Corp Pref C	AES C	1.00	6.80%
El Paso Pref C	EP C	1.00	5.20%
Conn Lt & Power	CNLPL	1.00	6.10%

Treasury Inflation Protected Bonds

Company	Ticker Symbol	Beta	Yield
Vanguard	VIPSX	0.00	1.49

Cash Account

Company	Beta	Yield
Savings Bonds, EE	0.00	3.1%
Vanguard Muni MM	0.00	0.4%
Vanguard Prime MM	0.00	0.3%
Bank of America CDs	0.00	0.8%

Total Portfolio Beta   = 0.56
Total Portfolio Yield   = 6.70%
Total Portfolio Return = 12.26%

Notice that the beta and yields of the original and most recent portfolios are close. This was achieved by design and maintaining control on the buying and selling of positions in increments, which leads us to the next section.

Incremental Buying

Averaging your investments on an incremental basis will give you the best prospect of assembling a portfolio that will exceed market returns. By using this approach, it is most likely that we won't buy at the highs nor buy at the lows. We will only buy when a target range presents itself. Make your incremental stock purchases periodically, according to the investment plan you determined in Chapter 3. Base your stock purchases on facts and not emotions or market swings. Buying on the facts will also reinforce the effect of averaging your portfolio acquisition price-per-share. Do set buy-limit orders to enter stocks you want to own, but keep up with the underlying company's prospects.

Target Buy Range

How do we know that we are in the target range for our stock?

The target range determination selection process will use the financial resources mentioned in the Chapter 11 homework section, such as Yahoo Finance, Street.com, or Bloomberg.com. Personally, I use Yahoo Finance as my primary resource, due to its simplicity. It has more info listed on a one-page summary than most other sites, and with the links provided for more detailed information. Although Yahoo Finance is an excellent source, you should periodically compare the financial summary results with other sources. This ensures that you are using the most up-to-date information.

On the summary page of Yahoo Finance, you will find that a lot of the homework has been already completed for you. I didn't want to mention it earlier because you need to know how to figure out the elementary fundamentals of potential investments. In other words, you need to be able to determine whether a company is a candidate for the investment of your hard-earned dollars. When it is your dollars at stake facts not emotions are the rule.

To keep you from becoming overwhelmed or bogged down by analyzing financial information, an outline of our step-by-step process of qualifying your stock pick is listed below for you. As mentioned earlier, you will find that the number-crunching aspect has been compiled. You just need to know what to look for and where to look for it. When you access the summary page, start by making sure that you have the correct company and most importantly, the correct ticker symbol that will be used in buying the stock.

Then look at the previous close and the day's opening price, which will result in that particular day's trading range. How does the price look in comparison to the 52-week trading range? If we are inside the band of the 52-week trading range, then we have a viable candidate so far. Moving down the page, take a look at today's volume and compare it to the average volume (usually three months trailing average). Is there more or less than the average volume for today's trading activity? If volume is higher than the average, recheck the news headlines to see what types of announcements have been made that are impacting the company. Check the amount of the dividends the stock is paying and how often it is paid. Yahoo Finance lists the dollar amount and the annual percentage yield. Although Yahoo Finance does a good job of keeping the yield information updated throughout the day, you should check it by taking the dollar amount of the yield and dividing it by the stock price. This will produce the annual dividend yield.

Next, check to see when and how the dividend payments are being made. If the dividends are paid monthly or, most likely quarterly, take the next step. If the dividend is paid annually or on some other unusual payment terms, then stop, do not pass go! The Preferred Way strategy only invests in stocks that pay monthly or quarterly dividends. The reasoning is that a lot of things can go wrong while waiting for a dividend that is paid out only once a year. While we are long-term in outlook, we don't want to be in a situation where a long time is required to get paid for the risk that is being taken. In other words, we want our dividends and gains sooner rather later, so that the power of compounding can work for us. This is why our strategy calls for you to get paid monthly or quarterly, which helps offset in the risk of capital loss. Warren Buffet's first three rules of "Do Not Lose Principal" apply.

Then, look down the column and find the Price-to-Earnings (PE) and Earnings-Per-Share (EPS). Check the earnings-per-share against the analyst's opinion listing. Is the company on track to meet or exceed quarterly and annual estimates? If the answer is yes, then compare the price-to-earnings to the industry competitor comparisons. If the company is in line with the competition, then we will advance to the next decision. If the answer is no, then check to see the cause. It could be something as simple as the company undertaking a larger capital spending plan to develop or improve existing properties.

Next, let's take a look at the analyst's estimates. While we do not depend upon the analysts to make our decision for us, it can offer reassurance that we are on the right track if there are a majority of buy ratings. Conversely, it can provide us with a warning if there are a number of underperform or sell ratings. If there are recent changes in the analyst's opinion of a sell rating, then heed this warning and recheck the news. If all else fails, call the analyst if you really need to. The analyst most likely will not take your call, but one of his associates may be able to bring more light on the movement. Do not abuse your ability to call the analyst, but when all else fails, give it a try. Also, call the company investor relations department and ask them about what is causing the downgrade movements. If your pick has survived this gauntlet of checks, then it is a very good candidate for purchase.

One last thing to check out. Take a look at the order position tab and see the top of the order book (who's next) in either the buy or ask queue. Yahoo Finance currently offers the order book information in real-time. Hopefully, the order book pricing is close to what you want to pay and can serve to confirm your purchase price.

You are now ready to buy your stock! If you are using an on-line broker, then have your screen ready to go once you have selected your entry-level price point. Do not stall. If your stock is in the price band and qualifies, then go ahead and click the mouse and complete the transaction. Remember to use limit orders at a slight discount to the asking price. If you have chosen to order through your broker, then make sure that the order is taken for your correct pricing parameters, utilizing limit orders. Would you pay full retail unless you absolutely had to? The same applies in buying stock. It can prove exasperating at times, but overall you will come out ahead. Occasionally, you may have to pay full retail or slightly more, but if you don't ask for a discount, the market will not give you one.

Reinvest the Dividends and Capital Gains

One of the best reasons for reinvesting dividends and capital gains is that it compounds your dividend payouts. Reinvesting gets you more shares, so your future dividends also rise, as long as the company does not cut the payout. The power of compounding comes into effect and can propel your investment to more income and wealth in the future. You will be pleasantly surprised with the results after a year or more of dividend reinvestment. Remember the power of compound discussion in Chapter 2? Einstein and Warren Buffet stated that the time value of compounding is a powerful force and I think that we should remember this. If you are funding your portfolio via an IRA or 401-K, then you will not have to worry about filing or amending your tax return.

Create Your Paycheck

You have now completed our stock selection process and have dividends and capital gains set on reinvest. However, there is another point that needs to be considered. Doesn't the thought of creating a steady source of income sound great? If you have followed the tenants of the Preferred Way Basic Training and the stock selection rules in the Chapter 12, then you have selected a portfolio of lower-risk dividend-producing stocks. It is now time to consider when these dividends are scheduled to be paid. You know from the Chapter 12 qualifying process when and on what frequency the stocks are to pay dividends. You can also double-check this information on the Yahoo finance summary page. If your dividend payments are monthly, there are no other considerations to be made on this.

If dividends are paid quarterly, determine whether the quarter end is on a March, June, July, December sequence, a January, April, July, November sequence or other such quarterly sequence. You may want to try to select your investments so that the dividend payouts are not received all in one quarter end sequence. In other words, try to have some dividends being paid on the January quarter sequence and some payments on the March quarter sequence. This will help you avoid a "lumpy" payment stream.

By avoiding the lumpy payments, it will help you work through volatile markets, while reinvesting your dividends. It is more comforting to receive these funds on a steady basis. Dividend payments aren't immune to the volatility and they aren't as stable as cash in a certificate of deposit. You must also consider that cash won't pay you 5%, 6%, or even 7% or more year-after-year, nor will it give you the chance to make as solid a capital gain as the alternative.

This step is entirely optional, but it can help protect you during times when the market is volatile by reinvesting your dividend during down periods, which will result in more shares purchased, thereby adding more income to achieve your goals.

Prune Your Portfolio Periodically

As a part of your ongoing portfolio-monitoring process, you must always be on the lookout for items that negatively impact your investment. If you determine that the investment no longer meets the rigors of the investment-qualifying process or the reported news is negative, then you must be prepared to sell. Always keep a "short list" of stocks that were not as attractive as the stocks you purchased. This will help save you time if and when a replacement to your portfolio is needed.

Reminder

Most brokerage firms will provide you with information on how much per share you have paid. This is called a cost basis. It is the number that you need to offset when your broker reports a sale of a stock to the IRS. The IRS receives the sell number and as far as it is concerned, it is the amount that you realized from the stock sale. At tax time you need the cost basis of your stock to offset what the IRS thinks is the full proceeds.

You may have a gain or a loss from the result of this simple subtraction process, but you must report it accurately. If you made five purchases of a stock over a six-month to six-year time frame and had your capital gains and dividends reinvested in the stock as received, then you need to know the cost basis or the cost of amount invested over these time frames.

The compounding of the capital gains and dividends complicates the cost basis calculation and, although it is not a hard calculation, it can be very tedious. For this reason, when selecting a broker, whether a person or online, make sure that they provide this service to you at no cost. It will save you a lot of time and trouble when you sell an investment. It is extremely important to keep an eye on this process so that you will not have any surprises when tax time rolls around.

Chapter 13: Boring is Beautiful

Remember that the money managers appearing on financial networks and other media are institutional or large-money investors. They have a different stake in the game. They are being paid big bucks to perform daily. You must remember that you are an individual investor. Your challenge is to not go to sleep at the wheel. You must continue to monitor your portfolio on a regular basis. Don't take your eyes off your portfolio. Keep a vigilant watch over the stocks that you have chosen. After all, iIt is your hard-earned money, after all.

As individual investors, we are content to receive our dividends while waiting on our companies to produce capital gains for us. Preferred Way investors look for companies who have business models and plans that are easy to understand and generate a lot of cash. Our emotions aren't impacted by the market-inspired panic mode because we have a well-thought-out plan.

This may not sound as exciting as day-trading tech stocks or currency futures, but we are preserving and growing our wealth over time, with a sustainable strategy. Preferred Way investors like predictability. We like to be paid dividends that a company pays in cash. Although nothing is guaranteed, you have a low beta portfolio and are no longer subject to the roller coaster ride of the daily market.

Next-Generation Investments

If boring is beautiful, then why is the topic of next-generation investments being addressed here? Because, as investors receiving a comfortable income stream and enjoying capital gains, we must not become complacent.

Other industry segments must be investigated to determine if, in the future, they could become part of our portfolio. Perhaps these new industries or companies could form an entire asset allocation segment, fitting into our allocation framework in addition to or as part of our five asset classes.

Will other industries become a part of the Preferred Way asset mix in the future? Answering this question becomes a bit easier for Preferred Way investors. We are looking for companies that pay dividends and have a great free cash flow. I am not thinking about investing in the next SpaceX, no offense to Mr. Branson. I am thinking of investing in undervalued or not-heavily-followed market sectors that meet our current qualifying criteria. You remember how we assembled our portfolio? The same thinking is required to qualify investments.

This leads us to think about the water business. The water and sewage businesses are vastly under-appreciated by the market. As more municipalities subcontract out their water and sewage systems, the water sector is becoming more consolidated by companies who have achieved the scale to drive costs well below what a local government or agency can accept to manage the business. Water is a prime necessity, far more important and imperative in terms of importance when compared to a lot of other industries. Without water, life cannot be sustained. The United States today has adequate supplies and operators. We need to keep a close eye on this business domestically because it can yield major investment opportunities that meet our qualifying criteria.

Water companies are responsible for distributing fresh water throughout towns and cities, piping it into buildings and removing and treating sewage. Most water companies are owned or run by local municipalities. The scarcity of water in parts of the country and throughout the world is transitioning from a small issue to a wide-scale problem. Supplies are expected to tighten, providing earnings potential as demand exceeds supply.

Several of these companies, such as Aqua America and American Water Works, certainly aren't household names, yet. Through aggregation and consolidation they are carving out a huge business for themselves. Water and sewage facilities are in short supply in many third world nations and they will require better water facilities as their populations increase. You will find there are several worldwide operators that meet most of our criteria. It is recommended that investors keep an eye on domestic U.S. companies and not the foreign-based companies. Our accounting standards and media coverage is much better than what most of the foreign operators are subject to.

Many sources are pointing to solar as the next big clean energy replacement for coal and petroleum-based products. In the long run, they will probably be right, but for now, without tax credits and state and federal subsidies, the profitability of the companies is still somewhat doubtful. Our qualifying criteria demands that companies generate a strong free cash flow and have the ability to pay dividends. Solar companies don't fit the mold, yet. Not to end on a down note, there is huge potential for this business but not at the current cost and demand on structures in place.

Natural gas has been covered in the energy section portfolio, but the upside potential has not been realized by the end-user market or the investor community. The

U.S is on its way to becoming a net exporter of natural gas and natural gas-related products. This will substantially ramp up demand for exploration and transport of natural gas products. It is mentioned here because the potential for market expansion in the U.S. and internationally is huge. Allocations to the portfolio may have to be changed if the natural gas market can achieve its potential. Keep this in mind as you move forward in the periodic monitoring of your investments.

Keeping the environment clean is an important upward trend. Companies that provide waste cleanup solutions to the industrial and energy production sectors will see their revenues ramp up as the U.S. economy shifts its consumption of coal and crude oil to natural gas. Companies are exploiting fuel cell technologies that were initially developed and utilized by NASA for its Mars missions. One company in particular, Bloom Energy has an impressive customer list, with companies like Coca-Cola, Walmart and FedEx are currently using their fuel cells to reduce their electricity consumption. Just think of the amount of electricity an entire farm of Bloom Energy fuel cells could save!

New solutions will need to be developed and old mind sets overcome in order to deliver and utilize cheaper and more available forms of energy production. This could be a paradigm shift for the U.S. economy just as technology was in the 1990s. These huge shifts in the way America thinks about powering itself in a prudent fashion will create investment opportunities on the scale of tech during the late 1990's. There will be a lot of money made by the pioneering visionaries and investors alike.

Chapter 14: Are We There Yet?

You must act on fulfilling your financial goals today. No matter what you tell yourself, if you do not act now, while this information is fresh in your mind, then the odds are that you will use only part of the information or maybe not invest at all.

I implore you to act immediately so that you can obtain a more comfortable lifestyle and not have the day-to-day financial worries that most others have. It doesn't matter whether you have one thousand or tens of thousands of dollars, you have to overcome inertia and gain momentum now. Just think. No more financial planning so you can swing a vacation or make that tuition payment for your kids. The Preferred Way strategy was devised to help you realize those dreams of early retirement or to enjoy lifetime events with your family. Are we there yet?

Preferred Way investors like predictability. We like to be paid dividends that a company pays in cash. Although nothing is guaranteed, you have assembled a low-beta portfolio and have eliminated a lot of the worry generated by the roller coaster gyrations of the market. It is hard to stay disciplined when the media pundits are continually offering distractions. You must try to resist. The Preferred Way discipline dictates that you pay little attention to TV shows with multiple ticker crawlers moving across the screen. The anchors sound as if they could be calling a ball game. The reason for this is that they not only must capture your attention but hold it for extended periods. This is accomplished by making what seems to be constant "calls" on the market. The market is up, it's down, and so it goes for the rest of the day.

Can you imagine watching a basketball game during which the announcers give only a summary of the action every 10 or 15 minutes? There would be a lot of channel-changers. With the basketball announcers' play-by-play and commentary, they are able to maintain our interest and even help provide the viewer with more excitement with Dick Vitale-type punctuations such as "whoops" or "crashing the boards baby." The financial TV anchors provide a similar commentary such as "the markets down, it's really going down" or "we are now moving higher." They have a vested interest in keeping your attention so that you won't change the channel. Then a guest host, professional analyst or trader is brought in to explain to us mere mortals what the catalysts are behind the market movements and how to play the market. The market usually winds up playing the traders. We don't play the market; we coexist and collect our dividends and capital gains.

The financial news anchors and their guest market professionals know that it is very hard to beat the market on a short-term basis. Take a look at their performance records. These market professionals are paid big bucks to express their opinions and pick stocks for their firms. The firm's brokers then sell to their clients and make a lot of money for the firm and themselves. Hence the adage, "If you listen to a broker, you will become just that, broker." About one half of these market professionals don't even match the market bench mark returns of the S&P 500 or the Dow index, as their performance records indicate.

Unless you are a hedge fund, high-frequency or a large capital trader dealing in very small pricing movements driven by a main frame computer, you will not be able to capture price movements as efficiently as the larger players. It can be nerve-wracking to follow stock price movements for 15 minutes, much less for a couple of hours. Heck, if nothing else it makes me nervous and probably you also.

Prudently review your investments on a periodic basis. Pay attention to the companies in your portfolio. Do not get distracted by the talking heads on TV.

You can't predict what your carefully chosen investments will do. If you could, then you would be sitting on your private island. Think long-term. The U.S. economy has been remarkably resilient. Most importantly, you will be able to earn safe returns over long periods of time with your low beta portfolio. During turbulent times, remember that you use electricity and water daily. Unfortunately, we are still using oil almost daily. As we pointed out earlier, don't try and outsmart the market.

You are now positioned to collect your dividend paychecks, reinvest proceeds and you are doing so with about half the risk of the S&P 500. Maintain diligence on your financial plan and monitor your goals as we discussed earlier.

Just by reading this book you're ahead of 90% of other investors. By creating your plan and portfolio, you are ahead of 99% of other investors. Use this head start to your advantage. If you haven't started assembling your portfolio, begin today. When others say that you will fail, stick to you plan and continue one step at a time and you will arrive at your goal. Best regards to you and your family.

Web Resources

Yahoo!
  www.finance.yahoo.com

Bloomberg
  www.bloomberg.com

CNBC
  www.cnbc.com

CalcXML
  www.financialcalculators.com

Motley Fool
  www.fool.com

Wallstreet Journal
  www.marketwatch.com

Jim Cramer Affiliate
  www.street.com

U. S. Treasury Department
  www.treasurydirect.com

Federal Reserve Board
  www.federalreserve.com

The Yield Hunter (Preferred Stocks)
  www.dividendyieldhunter.com

Preferred Way
  www.thepreferredway.com

Web Resources

Bankrate.com
www.bankrate.com

Select Online Brokers

Fidelity
www.fidelity.com

Vanguard
www.vanguard.com

TIPS Providers

Vanguard
877-662-7447

Fidelity
800-343-3548

Definitions

Annual Report: An annual report is issued by publicly-traded companies once a year. The annual report conveys the company's financial performance and activities of the previous year. The annual report includes financial highlights and reports company operations.

Ask Price: This is the price point at which shareholders are willing to sell shares of their stock.

Asset Allocation: The amount of an investor's money invested in different asset types, such as stocks, cash, or other securities. Each incremental investment type is expressed as a percentage of each type of investment. All of the incremental allocations add up to 100%. This method of allocation serves as a guide or blueprint to keep an investor on track to reach established goals. It defines a path for an investor to balance the desire for a high return, while assuming low-risk.

Balance Sheet: The portion of a financial statement that accounts for a company's assets and liabilities at a certain point in time.

Beta: This is a mathematical measure of a stock's risk as compared to an overall market or market segment. Typically, a stock with a beta equal to 1.0 has the same amount of mathematical risk as the market to which the stock is being compared. A stock with a beta equal to 0.50 implies risk equal to one half of the market it is being compared to.

Bid Price: The highest price that a buyer is willing to pay for a stock.

Capital Gains: When a stock is sold for an amount over its original cost, its said to generate a capital gain (a profit). If a stock is sold below its original cost, then the difference is a capital loss.

Capital Preservation: An investment method that serves to protect the principal amounts invested.

Certificate of Deposit: Also known as CDs. This is a certificate issued that indicates a certain amount of money has been deposited earning a rate over a certain period of time.

Common Stock: A security that represents a share of equity ownership in a company. They also may provide the holder with a share of the company's profits via a dividend distribution.

Credit Risk: A probability or possibility measurement used to predict if a company will enter into a default on its obligations to pay.

Day Order: An offer to buy a security that is good only for the day in which it is placed.

Diversification: The process of dividing a portfolio's investment funds among a variety of securities that are of different risk levels in order to minimize overall risk of the portfolio.

Dividends: Refers to periodic payments that companies pay out to their shareholders. These dividend payouts represent a portion of the company's earnings being returned to the shareholders of the business.

Dividend Reinvestment Plans: Also known as DRIP or DRIPS. These investment plans allow an investor to purchase shares without a brokerage account by buying directly from the company or its agents. The company usually does not charge the investor for providing this service. A key advantage of the DRIP is that shareholders can acquire shares over long periods of time using dollar cost averaging at no additional cost.

Dollar Cost Averaging: This is a methodical investing strategy that requires that the investor put money to work each month or quarter. By averaging stock purchases over a long period of time, this method insures that the investor will not purchase the stock at the worst time in the market. In a sense, this is a form of diversification in that the stock purchase cost is averaged out.

Equity or Equities: These terms usually refer to a stock.

Free Cash Flow: Also referred to as FCF. This is the amount of cash that a company has available after all its financial obligations and capital expenditures are met. The higher a company's FCF, the more financial flexibility it has.

Income Statement: Also referred to as a profit and loss statement. It states the profitability of a company by consolidating the various sources of income and subtracting the costs associated with generating the income.

Index: A gauge or benchmark of performance of the financial markets or its subsets. An example of an index is the S&P 500 or the Dow Jones Industrial Average.

Leverage: Also referred to and known as gearing. The use of debt instruments to increase expected returns more than what could otherwise be afforded by a company.

Limit Order: An order that allows the investor to set the price at which a security is to be bought or sold.

Liquidity: The ability to readily sell an asset easily.

Master Limited Partnership: Often referred to as MLP or MLPs. These are partnership securities that trade like stocks, with the difference being that the holder of the partnership unit is referred to as a partner or unit holder.

Market Order: An order given to buy or sell immediately at the best available price.

Money Market Account: An account that pays interest on short interest rates, typically higher than a savings account, and are FDIC insured.

Money Market Mutual Funds: An account that invests in short-term debt and is considered a liquid cash asset. These accounts usually pay out more than the bank money market accounts, but are not FDIC insured.

Net Income: A company's total amount of revenues generated from all sources minus the cost of doing business, interest expenses, taxes, and other costs. It is also referred to as the bottom line, as it is the final line of an income statement.

Price-to-Earnings: Current stock price divided by the earnings or expected earnings generated by a company. Expressed as current stock price/earnings per share = price earnings ratio or P/E ratio.

Rebalancing: The act of periodically adjusting the proportions of assets within an investment portfolio, as needed. It is recommended to Preferred Way investors to rebalance quarterly. The rebalancing strategy is to sell portions of assets that have risen higher than established portfolio guidelines and use those proceeds to invest other assets within the portfolio or acquire new assets.

Return on Equity: Also known as ROE and refers to a company's earnings in proportion to its shareholder equity. The higher an ROE, the more profitable a company is. This is a useful tool to compare profitability between companies of different sizes and industries.

S&P 500 Index: A benchmark that measures the performance of the 500 largest capitalized companies in the U.S. stock market. It is considered to the best gauge of company performance across the broad U.S. market.

Statement of Cash Flow: This financial statement tracks the inflows and outflows of a company's money. It is one of the major financial statements that a publically traded company must provide to regulators and shareholders on a regular basis.

Stock: Stocks represent a shareholders partial ownership interest in a company and are also known as equities.

Treasury Inflation Protected Securities: Commonly referred to as TIPS and is a U.S. government-issued bond, if which the principal value is adjusted on a regular basis to reflect the impact of inflation over time. Unlike other types of bonds, TIPs do not deteriorate from the risk of inflation.

About the Author

Bill Orr, III is the Managing Director of Trimont Financial Services, a financial consulting firm based in Charlotte, North Carolina. Mr. Orr has worked with Trimont since 2004. Prior to 2004, he served as a Managing Director of GMAC Commercial Finance Group (2 years) and as a Managing Director of Bank of America Capital Funding Group (10 years).

Mr. Orr has experience in a wide array of financing for a diverse domestic and international client base. He has closed more than US $3.0 billion of transactions during his career and has an extensive network of contacts at major banks, investment banks, hedge funds, and private equity firms for syndication placement of a variety of financial products.

Prior to Bank of America, he served as Senior Investment Officer with Westinghouse Credit Corporation and as Vice President of Credit Management with Barclays Bank. Mr. Orr has won awards for Best Marketing, Highest Team Production, New Product Introduction, International Sales, and Transaction of the Year. He belongs to numerous financial and management associations. Mr. Orr earned a BSBA from Winthrop University.

17318484R00092

Made in the USA
Middletown, DE
18 January 2015